# Paul McCartney

## The Songs He Was Singing
## Vol.1
## The Seventies

# Paul McCartney
# The Songs He Was Singing
# Vol. 1
# The Seventies

JOHN BLANEY

**Paper Jukebox**

First published in 2003
Revised edition first published 2010

# Contents

# Introduction

When I began *Paul McCartney: The Songs He Was Singing* the best part of ten years ago, little did I think that I'd still be working on it all these years later. The book began to take shape in the summer of 1999. I'd recently graduated from Camberwell College of Art and wanted something to keep the little grey cells ticking over before diving back into the heady world of academia at Goldsmiths College the following year. A McCartney discography seemed like a good idea. I could combine what I'd learnt at Camberwell with my longstanding interest in McCartney's solo recording career.

At the time, the only McCartney discography available was in *The Beatles: Working Class Heroes* by John Tobler and Neville Stannard, and that only went as far as the early 1980s. If I wanted a comprehensive discography, I'd have to write it myself. So began a musical and literary journey that occupies me to this day.

It took about three years to finish the first draft, but despite McCartney's standing as one of the most popular and important musicians ever, few publishers showed interest. By the time a publisher eventually did offer me a deal, I'd already decided to self-publish.

The first edition was published in 2003 and sold out in six months. I thought about reprinting, but got sidetracked by my second book, *John Lennon: Listen To This Book*. I'd learnt a lot and *Listen To This Book* was a significant improvement on *Songs He Was Singing*. Apart from being better written and edited, it looked better because I realised that what a discography needs as much as text is illustrations.

With *Listen To This Book* out, my thoughts returned to reprinting *Songs He Was Singing*. Once again, I began looking for a publisher. My original goal was a simple reprint with more illustrations, but when Jawbone Press expressed an interest, all that changed. Jawbone wanted to publish both books ('Songs' and 'Listen') in a single volume, which they did as *Lennon and McCartney: Together Alone*. Jawbone did a great job, but as good as it was it still didn't have the illustrations I knew it needed.

That's changed with this new edition of *Paul McCartney: The Songs He Was Singing*. Fully revised and updated, it now includes as many illustrations as I could squeeze in. The only problem was that with all the revisions, updates and illustrations, it clocked in at over 800 pages. The obvious solution was to issue four volumes, one for each decade of McCartney's solo career.

It's been a long time coming, but I think I've finally achieved my original vision, and in glorious colour throughout. So here it is, *Paul McCartney: The Songs He Was Singing Vol. 1 The Seventies*. I hope you enjoy it.

# 1967-'70: Family Way to McCartney

'LOVE IN THE OPEN AIR' / 'THE FAMILY WAY'
GEORGE MARTIN & HIS ORCHESTRA
UK release December 23 1966; United Artists UP 1165; failed to chart.

'LOVE IN THE OPEN AIR' / 'BAHAMA SOUND'
GEORGE MARTIN & HIS ORCHESTRA
US release April 24 1967; United Artists UA 50148; failed to chart.

'Love In The Open Air' (McCartney)
'The Family Way' (McCartney)
Both with George Martin (conductor), The George Martin Orchestra (violins, violas, double bass). Both probably recorded at Abbey Road Studios, London, England. Both produced by A.I.R. (London).

'LOVE IN THE OPEN AIR' / 'THE FAMILY WAY'
THE TUDOR MINSTRELS
UK release December 23 1966; Decca F 12536; failed to chart.

'Love In The Open Air' (McCartney)
'The Family Way' (McCartney)
Both with Neville Marriner (conductor), The Tudor Minstrels (drums, basses, guitars, organ, trumpets, trombones, flutes, oboes, violins, violas, cellos). Both recorded at CTS Studios, London, England. Both produced, supervised, and orchestrated by George Martin.

*THE FAMILY WAY*
ORIGINAL SOUNDTRACK RECORDING
UK release January 6 1967; Decca LK 4847 (mono), SKL 4847 (stereo); failed to chart.
US release April 24 1967; LP London M 76007 (mono), MS 82007 (stereo); stereo reel-to-reel tape LPL-70136 (Ampex black box); 4-track cartridge LFX 17136 (white shell, front and back artwork); 8-track cartridge LE 72136 (white shell, front and back artwork); failed to chart.

'LOVE IN THE OPEN AIR'
McCartney's first solo project outside of The Beatles was a commission to write incidental music for a film made by the Boulting Brothers. Having recently quit touring, McCartney, Like Lennon, was looking for something to occupy him before The Beatles' began recording again in December. "It was most unglamorous really. I rang our NEMS office and said I would like to write a film theme; not a score, just a theme. John was away filming, so I had time to do it. NEMS fixed it for me to do the theme of 'The Family Way," McCartney told the *NME*.

Although it was Paul's project, it was originally reported as a joint Lennon and McCartney venture. *NME* reported in October: "When he returns from filming in Spain next month, John Lennon will help his songwriting partner Paul McCartney to score the new Hayley Mills film, *All In Good Time*. ... The picture's alternative working title of *Wedlocked* has now been dropped, the producers having settled on *All In Good Time*. Paul is believed to be already working on the music."

McCartney had been given a brief synopsis of the story and had indeed written a theme. When Lennon returned to Britain, he set about recording demos of the song he'd written while in Spain, 'Strawberry Fields Forever'. McCartney was also focusing on The Beatles next album and had to be pressured by George Martin to write a second theme for the film. Martin needed more from McCartney if he was going to score an entire soundtrack. Speaking to *NME* in December, Martin said: "I went to America for a time and, on returning [probably November 21st], realised we needed a love theme for the centre of the picture, something wistful. I told Paul and he said he'd compose something. I waited, but nothing materialised, and finally I had to go round to Paul's house and literally stand there until he'd composed something. John was visiting and advised a bit, but Paul created the tune and played it to me on guitar. I listened and wrote it down. It is a fragile, yet compelling, melody. I arranged it for woodwinds and strings, and we called it 'Love In The Open Air'. It's quite haunting."

With two McCartney themes to work with, George Martin wrote 13 variations, to be recorded by session musicians. Work progressed at lightning speed. Martin wrote the arrangements, hired the session musicians, led by Neville Marriner, and recorded the music – all within three weeks.

Although he had to be cajoled by Martin, McCartney wrote two contrasting themes that illustrate his instinctive sense of melody. Each has a distinctive mood conveyed with graceful eloquence. 'Love In The Open Air' is mellifluous and romantic; 'The Family Way' is brazen and resolute. Arranged by Martin, they proved to be remarkably adaptable and won McCartney an Ivor Novello Award for Best Instrumental Theme.

### 'Love In The Open Air' data
Decca was contracted to issue the recordings as an LP, but it also planned to issue a single (F12536). Martin objected, arguing that the versions recorded for the Decca LP were not commercial enough for release as a 45. He insisted that both melodies be re-recorded and made plans to issue his own recordings as a single (UP 1165). Decca was forced to postpone the release of the LP until Martin had completed his recordings for United Artists. Both set of recordings were released on Friday January 6 1967. The American pressing of Martin's single (UA 50148) offered an alternative edit and B-side ('Bahama Sound', a Martin composition). 'Love In The Open Air' was also recorded by Sounds Sensational with The Mike Sammes Singers and issued in America by Capitol (5957). A version by The Casino Royales was issued on the B-side of 'When I Tell You (That I Love You)' London (HLU 10122) in March 1967. The single was issued in America by Coliseum Records (45-2707).

In Britain, Decca issued *The Family Way* LP in stereo (SKL 4847) with blue and silver labels and in mono (LK 4847) with red and sliver labels. In America, London issued *The Family Way* LP in stereo (MS 82007) and in mono (M 76007). The London LP was issued with a different cover to the British edition. Some copies of the London LP were issued with stickers fixed to the front cover to denote that they were demonstration copies, not for sale. *The Family Way* soundtrack was issued in Canada on CD by Disques XXI-21 Records on July 22 2003, but the original 1966 recordings appear to have been mastered from a vinyl source (there are bonus recordings added by Carl Aubut and the Quatuor La Flute Enchantee, recorded in 1995 and 1998 respectively).

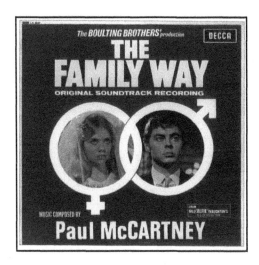

## 'THINGUMYBOB' / 'YELLOW SUBMARINE'
## BLACK DYKE MILLS BAND
UK **release** September 6 1968; Apple Records APPLE 4; failed to chart.
US **release** August 26 1968; Apple Records 1800; failed to chart.

### 'Thingumybob' (Lennon, McCartney)
### 'Yellow Submarine' (Lennon, McCartney)
Both with Black Dyke Mills Band (various brass instruments). Recorded at Victoria Hall, Exhibition Road, Saltaire. Both produced by Paul McCartney.

### 'THINGUMBYBOB'
Although it was credited to Lennon-McCartney, there can be little doubt that 'Thingumybob' was solely the work of McCartney. Had he written it two years earlier, it would have sat snugly alongside the two themes he written for *The Family Way*. Like 'Love In The Open Air' it was written as theme music, on this occasion to an ITV London Weekend Television comedy broadcast from August 2 to September 20, 1968.

McCartney asked his record producer, George Martin, to write the score for 'Thingumybob' and record it with the George Martin Orchestra (later issued on the *George Martin 50 Years Of Recording* boxed set). McCartney wasn't impressed with his producer's arrangement and travelled to Saltire, just north of Bradford, to record it and the B-side, 'Yellow Submarine' with the Black Dyke Mills Band. Recording took place both inside and outside of Victoria Hall, Exhibition Road, on June 30 with McCartney producing.

### 'Thingumybob' data
Apple issued 'Thingumybob' (APPLE 4) in Britain on September 6 and in America (1800) on August 26, 1968. The single was issued with generic Apple labels and paper sleeve. Two label variants were manufactured in America. The first has the text placed vertically on the label with the song credited to McCartney & Lennon and the full band name, John Foster & Sons Ltd Black Dyke Mills Band, on three lines. The second variant flips A- and B-sides placing 'Yellow Submarine' on the green A-side label.

## McCARTNEY
## PAUL McCARTNEY

**Side 1** 'The Lovely Linda', 'That Would Be Something', 'Valentine Day', 'Every Night', 'Hot As Sun – Glasses', 'Junk', 'Man We Was Lonely'.

**Side 2** 'Oo You', 'Momma Miss America', 'Teddy Boy', 'Singalong Junk', 'Maybe I'm Amazed', 'Kreen–Akore'.

**UK release** April 7 1970; LP Apple PCS 7102; 8-track cartridge Apple 8X-PCS 7102; mono reel-to-reel tape Apple TA-PMC 7102; chart high No.2.

**US release** April 20 1970; LP Apple STAO-3363; 8-track cartridge Apple 8XT3363; stereo reel-to-reel tape Apple L-3363; chart high No.1.

### 'The Lovely Linda' (McCartney)
Paul McCartney (vocals, guitar, bass, hand slaps). Recorded at home studio, Cavendish Avenue, London, England.

### 'That Would Be Something' (McCartney)
Paul McCartney (vocals, guitar, electric guitar, bass, tom tom, cymbal). Recorded at home studio, Cavendish Avenue; mixed at Abbey Road Studios, London, England.

### 'Valentine Day' (McCartney)
Paul McCartney (vocals, guitar, electric guitar, bass, drums). Recorded at home studio, Cavendish Avenue; mixed at Abbey Road Studios.

### 'Every Night' (McCartney)
Paul McCartney (vocals, guitar, bass, drums). Recorded at Abbey Road Studios.

### 'Hot As Sun / Glasses' (McCartney)
Paul McCartney (guitar, bass, keyboards, maracas, bongos, wineglasses, vocal, piano, drums). Recorded at Morgan Studios, London, England.

### 'Junk' (McCartney)
Paul McCartney (vocals, guitar, bass, xylophone, drums, Mellotron, piano), Linda McCartney (backing vocals). Recorded at home studio, Cavendish Avenue and Morgan Studios.

### 'Man We Was Lonely' (McCartney)
Paul and Linda McCartney (vocals, guitar, steel guitar, bass, drums), Linda McCartney (backing vocals). Recorded at Abbey Road Studios.

### 'Oo You' (McCartney)
Paul McCartney (vocals, guitar, bass, aerosol, tambourine, cow bell drums). Recorded at home studio, Cavendish Avenue and Morgan Studios.

### 'Momma Miss America' (McCartney)
Paul McCartney (vocals, guitar, bass, piano, drums). Recorded at home studio, Cavendish Avenue.

### 'Teddy Boy' (McCartney)
Paul McCartney (vocals, guitar, bass, drums), Linda McCartney (backing vocals). Recorded at home studio, Cavendish Avenue and Morgan Studios.

### 'Maybe I'm Amazed' (McCartney)
Paul McCartney (vocals, piano, keyboards, guitar, bass, drums), Linda McCartney (backing vocals). Recorded at Abbey Road Studios.

### 'Kreen-Akore' (McCartney)
Paul McCartney (vocals, guitar, piano, organ, bow & arrow, percussion, drums), Linda McCartney (backing vocals). Recorded at Morgan Studios.

All produced by Paul McCartney.

## McCARTNEY

Released a mere seven days after McCartney announced that he was leaving The Beatles, his eponymous debut was recorded as the most influential band in the world disintegrated around him. By the time *McCartney* was begun in September 1969, the end of The Beatles was nigh. Harrison and Starr had both quit the band but were coaxed back. Lennon had made his dissatisfaction known through a series of solo projects that included peace events, concerts, avant-garde records, and films. He'd even announced his intention to leave the band at an Apple board meeting but was persuaded to keep quiet by manager Allen Klein, who was renegotiating The Beatles' contract with EMI.

Brian Epstein's death in 1967 marked the beginning of the end of The Beatles. It started power struggles and infighting that dogged the group until its end and beyond. Lennon had once been the driving force, but as his relationship with Yoko Ono blossomed, he became increasingly distanced from the group. With Lennon committed to projects outside of The Beatles, McCartney took control and began directing its output. Eleven weeks after completing the mammoth *White Album*, The Beatles began work on another McCartney-influenced project, the back-to-basics *Get Back/Let It Be* film and record. Intended to pull The Beatles together, it effectively tore them apart. Coming too soon after the lengthy *White Album* sessions, *Get Back/Let It Be* was a disaster waiting to happen. It was described by George Harrison as "the low of all-time" and by John Lennon as "the shittiest load of badly recorded shit, with a lousy feeling toward it, ever". To say that The Beatles weren't getting on is an understatement.

Aligned with this ill feeling were growing business and management concerns. Apple, a conglomerate of companies designed to ease The Beatles' tax burden, was launched in 1968 as a kind of hippie business utopia. Needless to say, this egalitarian dream quickly turned sour. The group's desire to combine counterculture values (artistic freedom) with modern business practices (total control of their music and image rights) opened up a financial black hole that all but swallowed them whole. Derek Taylor, friend of The Beatles and Apple press officer, recalled: "They took on a lot with Apple. They took on business and pleasure and funding the arts, and did try to live up to some of their personal promises. There was a high quotient of sincerity in there, as well as a bit of madness."

Apple quickly metamorphosed from hippie utopia into chaotic business dystopia. Attempting to save their empire from ruin, Lennon called in notorious American businessman Allen Klein, who made drastic cutbacks in an attempt to stop the outward flow of cash. McCartney, however, was having none of this – not because he didn't want to put Apple on a stable business footing, but because he insisted on having his father-in-law, Lee Eastman, manage his business affairs.

By late summer 1969, even McCartney had had enough of working with The Beatles and began recording his debut solo album. Initially, he recorded at his London home using a Studer 4-track tape recorder borrowed from EMI. He opted for home recording for the privacy it afforded him and because he wanted to keep the album a secret from Apple and Klein. "It was in the middle of all the Beatles wrangles," McCartney explained. "And so what we had to do was we had to keep it all out of Apple in case somebody burned the negatives or burned the tapes. It was a bit political at the time. So we just kept it all out. Just booked the studios ourselves, didn't show anyone at Apple the cover. Got another guy in, a mate of ours, to do the cover. Linda shot that nice cover with the baby and the jacket and cherries on the other side."

When McCartney did record outside his home (at Morgan and Abbey Road Studios in London), sessions were booked either by Linda or using the pseudonym Billy Martin. "For two reasons, really: fun and privacy," he recalled. "I think there's a big character in American baseball called Billy Martin, so that's where the name came from."

The Beatles revelled in spontaneity, and much of what McCartney committed to tape was improvised in this spirit. But the instinctive outbursts of creativity he committed to tape, combined with the understated production, seemed out of character. Coming off the back of *Abbey Road*, the rough simplicity of *McCartney* was surprising. Reviewing the album for *Rolling Stone* magazine, Langdon Winner expressed just such a reaction. "In both the quality of its songs and the character of its production *McCartney* will no doubt be a disappointment to many Beatles fans. Most people probably hoped that Paul's album would be a gigantic leap 'beyond the Beatles,' a super mind-blowing extravaganza with songs which would make 'Hey Jude' and 'Let It Be' seem pale by comparison. This did not happen. When compared to the best of the Beatles' previous work, the songs on *McCartney* are distinctly second rate."

If people thought McCartney would carry on where The Beatles had left off they were wrong, he never envisaged his album as *Abbey Road Part Two*. "When *McCartney* came along I had all these rough things," he said, "and I liked them all and thought, well, they're rough, but they've got that certain kind of thing about them, so we'll leave it and just put it out." Had the public and critics heard the album in relation to the rough and ready *Let It Be*, rather than the sophisticated *Abbey Road*, it mightn't have come as such a shock. Both approaches to recording illustrate McCartney's musical sensibility. The song fragments employed for the 'Long Medley' on *Abbey Road* were carefully stitched together to create an exquisite sonic tapestry. The listener could easily be forgiven for not even noticing the seams. But when he began work on his first solo album McCartney simply nailed fragments together in a somewhat crude manner akin to the way The Beatles approached *Let It Be*, which revealed both the process of recording and the rough edges that they usually spent hours smoothing away. *McCartney* extends the back-to basics approach its maker applied to *Let It Be*, but rather than hide the work processes, he made them visible.

What really hampered McCartney was the lack of decent material. Because he'd provided songs for The Beatles, Mary Hopkin, and Badfinger, he was forced to rework unfinished songs and improvise others. Consequently, songs recorded for *McCartney* spanned more than a decade, and some weren't up to scratch. McCartney defended the album saying: "They were almost throwaways, you know? But that's why they were included. They weren't quite throwaways. That was the whole idea of the album: all the normal things that you record that are great and have all this atmosphere but aren't that good as recording or production jobs. Normally that stuff ends up with the rest of your demos, but all that stuff is often stuff I love."

Love it or not, the release of the *McCartney* album marked the beginning of a creative roller-coaster ride that fuelled accusations of creative decline. After years of working in a creative maelstrom like The Beatles, he had no one other than himself to turn to. Years after his split with Lennon, he admitted that he missed having someone to bounce ideas off. "I definitely did miss a collaborator, because even if you've written a thing on your own, it's handy to just take it along to someone. They only have to tell you it's great – that's all the collaboration you need sometimes. Whereas otherwise you're just still wondering if it's any good. It's always good to have a little check, [a] second opinion."

The album was knocked by the press because McCartney used the break up of The Beatles to promote it. McCartney promoted the album in the same way he'd made it, crudely. His surprise announcement was intended to generate as much publicity as possible and to ensure the press got the message he included an explicit press kit with advance copies of the album. "We're doing a kit with the album which is an information thing," McCartney told *Rolling Stone* magazine weeks before the album was released. "It should be nice to receive the way we're playing it. All the answers to this whole thing we're doing are really supposed to be on the record and what's going on around it." McCartney was planning to give The Beatles the biggest public kiss off ever.
In fact, if what McCartney told *Rolling Stone* was true, the entire *McCartney* album was one big adieu. The kit was only available with advance copies of the album distributed to the British and American media and its four pages of Q&A made it clear that he and The Beatles had parted company.

Q: Is this album a rest away from The Beatles or the start of a solo career?
A: Time will tell. Being a solo album means 'the start of a solo career' ... and not being done with The Beatles means it's a rest. So it's both.
Q: Are you planning a new album or single with The Beatles?
A: No.
Q: Is the break with The Beatles temporary or permanent, due to personal differences or musical ones?
A: Personal differences, business differences, musical differences, but most of all because I have a better time with my family. Temporary or permanent? I don't know.
Q: Do you foresee a time when Lennon-McCartney becomes an active songwriting partnership again?
A: No.

It's easy to forget how much publicity surrounded the release of the *McCartney* album. Some thought it reeked of hype and that using the break up of the most popular group on the planet to promote the album somehow tainted the music. Once again, Langdon Winner posed the question: "Most disturbing of all, however, are the four information sheets written for the album — sheets which, despite Paul's wishes, are not included in the American release. The sheets contain even more assertions about how happy and peaceful Paul and Linda are these days, and some interview statements from Paul concerning his relationship to the Beatles—statements which drip a kind of unsavoury vindictiveness. Although it is a painful question to ask, why did Paul choose to cover a very beautiful and pleasing record with such tawdry propaganda?"

The reason why McCartney chose to announce his departure from The Beatles using such tawdry propaganda was because his album was up against *Let It Be*, due for release on May 8. Having just left the group, McCartney was in no mood to be bettered by The Beatles. McCartney was asked to postpone his album for the good of the group by Ringo Starr who was dispatched to McCartney's London home with the request and duly sent away with a flea in his ear. McCartney wasn't going to change the release date of his album for anyone, and certainly not The Beatles.

## McCartney songs

The album opens with 'The Lovely Linda', an uncompleted fragment that McCartney suggested was "a trailer to the full song, which will be recorded in the future". Recorded as an experiment "with more concern for testing the [tape] machine than with anything else", it was issued as it stood, unfinished. McCartney had intended to finishing the song, but when interviewed in 2001, he admitted: "I was always going to finish it, and I had another bit that went into a Spanish song, almost mariachi, but it just appeared as a fragment and was quite nice for that reason."

The next track, 'That Would Be Something', was written in Scotland in 1969 and recorded at McCartney's London home. McCartney evokes the force of nature as a metaphor for his relationship with Linda. Watching her symbolically cleansed by "the falling rain", he imagines a moment of transcendence where Linda, the personification of natural beauty, becomes one with nature.

On 'Valentine Day', working on his own again, McCartney was forced to revisit a recording practice he first explored while making the *White Album*. McCartney, Lennon, and Harrison developed a way of using multi-track tape to record their own backing tracks without the assistance of the others. McCartney took the practice a stage further and developed it as a way of writing. Improvising without a preconceived melody or arrangement in mind, he could write and record new compositions on the spot. Letting his subconscious run free, he layered random impressions onto the multi-track tape, shaping his music without knowing where it would lead him.

Explaining the process to Paul Gambaccini, he said: "What I did was to just go into the studio each day and just start with a drum track. Then I built it up a bit without any idea of how the song was going to turn out. It's like a reverse way of working. After laying down the drum track I added guitars and bass, building up the backing track." Like Lennon, McCartney was exploring a form of creativity developed by earlier generations of artists, writers, and composers. However, unlike Lennon's adventures with the avant-garde, McCartney's remained melodic and accessible. Improvised at home, 'Valentine Day' was an exploration of nonconformist creative techniques, influenced by an interest in the avant-garde and the restraints under which it was recorded.

McCartney busked 'Every Night' while filming *Let It Be* at Twickenham Studios in January 1969 and finished it while on holiday in Greece. "This came from the first two lines which I've had for a few years," he said. They were added to in 1969 while in Greece (Benitses) on holiday.

A love song inspired by Linda, it finds McCartney struggling with his personal demons. Attempting to reconcile conflicting emotions, he considers his options. The easy choice, drink and drugs, is rejected in favour of the infinitely more fulfilling alternative, domesticity and Linda. Attempting to deal with his traumas, McCartney increasingly turned to songwriting as catharsis. Writing 'Every Night' transformed his neurosis into creative energy. Revealing a troubled mind, it hints at an increasing reliance on Linda as a stabilising presence in his life.

To relieve their boredom while making *Let It Be*, The Beatles often revisited their early repertoire, which was peppered with instrumentals like 'Hot As Sun'. Ad-libbing the piece while filming *Let It Be*, McCartney performed it in a droll Hawaiian style. It was, according to McCartney: "A song written in about 1958 or 9 or maybe earlier, when it was one of those songs you play now and then. The middle was added at Morgan Studios, where the track was recorded."

While at Morgan Studios, he cross-faded two unrelated pieces at the end: playing wine glasses, he created the atmospheric instrumental 'Glasses'; then, as a teaser, he edited onto the end an uncredited fragment of 'Suicide', a song written with Frank Sinatra in mind. "I wrote this song called 'Suicide' which was very cabaret," he explained. "It was murder! Horrible song!" Sinatra rejected it. "Apparently he thought it was an almighty piss take. 'No way!' he's supposed to have said to one of his people. 'Is this guy having me on?'" Bootleg recordings of the piano demo have since surfaced, but the brief nine-second snippet on *McCartney* is all that has been made commercially available. (McCartney eventually debuted 'Suicide' on the BBC's *Michael Parkinson Show*, recorded at BBC Television Studios, London, on December 2 1999 and broadcast the following day on BBC One.)

The finished track was, in effect, a sound collage comprising three disparate musical fragments recorded in different places at different times. While Lennon and Ono used sound collage as part of a political strategy, McCartney simply delights in being able to take different ideas and glue them together. Just as our thoughts leap from one subject to another, McCartney takes random ideas, ways of making music and arbitrary selected melodies and jump cuts them together to emphasize discontinuity. McCartney breaks with a convention that demands continuity of tempo and key to draw attention to the constructed nature of recording. Constructed using a laborious process of overdubbing and editing that created a whole from different parts, it's a metaphor for the way he recorded the entire album.

'Junk' was written during The Beatles' Indian sojourn at Rishikesh in the Himalayan foothills. On their return to Britain, they gathered at George Harrison's Esher home and made demo recordings of the songs they'd written while in India. Although McCartney intended to use 'Junk' for *Abbey Road*, it remained unused until resurrected for *McCartney*. (The Beatles' attempt at the song – almost identical to McCartney's solo version – was released in 1996 on The Beatles' *Anthology 3*.) He recorded two versions at home before adding more instrumentation at Morgan Studios. Take one appeared without vocals as 'Singalong Junk'; take two had vocals. Its inclusion as an instrumental is superfluous and points to McCartney's struggle to find enough material to complete the album.

As concise a piece of self-analysis as anything Lennon wrote for his *Plastic Ono Band* album, McCartney's 'Man We Was Lonely' was, like Lennon's 'Hold On', influenced by the pain he experienced at the break-up of The Beatles. While it was born out of trauma, he nevertheless sees a resolution to his anxieties. His life-affirming refrain echoes Lennon's cries of self-realisation and suggests independence. Unlike Lennon, who exposed his vulnerability to the world, McCartney masks his with bravado and an upbeat musical support, which nevertheless reveals an exposed sensibility.

Part self-analysis, part defiant response, 'Man We Was Lonely' was a forthright piece of self-assurance, a celebration of having weathered the storm. As a considered message of intent, which informed the world (but more importantly Lennon and Ono) that Paul and Linda were doing just fine on their own, the song was a result of McCartney's alienation. Yet he turned this to his advantage, steeling his resolve to succeed and strengthen his relationship with Linda. Speaking to *Life* in April 1971, he said: "As a married couple, Linda and I've really become closer because of all those problems, all the decisions. It's been very real what I've been through, a breath of air, in a way, because of having been through very inhuman things." According to its author, 'Man We Was Lonely' "was written in bed at home, shortly before we finished recording the album. The middle was done one lunchtime in a great hurry as we were due to record the song that afternoon". Twelve takes were attempted at Abbey Road on February 25 1970, with McCartney completing overdubs and mixing at the same seven-hour session.

'Oo You' was improvised at home and, originally an instrumental, was "given lyrics one day after lunch, just before we left for Morgan Studios, where it was finished that afternoon". While at Morgan Studios, he copied his 4-track tape onto 8-track so that he could make more overdubs. With the extra space this made available, he added guitar, percussion, and an aerosol spray (panned hard right). The addition of lyrics gives the piece substance, but 'Oo You' remains little more than a well-disguised throwaway.

'Momma Miss America' too was ad-libbed at home and consists of two separate pieces joined together, with a sloppy edit marking the join. Like the other improvised instrumentals recorded for *McCartney*, it's proficient but not inspired. While recording *Get Back/Let It Be*, The Beatles churned out this kind of improvised material by the hour, and almost all of it remains unreleased – with good reason.

While they were filming *Let It Be*, Lennon, McCartney, and Harrison showcased a number of songs that later appeared on their solo albums. Lennon performed songs that appeared on *Imagine*. Harrison played songs destined for *All Things Must Pass*. McCartney previewed songs that were issued on *McCartney* and *Ram*. Like much of McCartney's material recorded for the ill-fated project, 'Teddy Boy' was sabotaged by Lennon. Programmed by Glyn Johns for The Beatles' *Get Back* album, the song was dropped from the running order when Phil Spector was called in to salvage the project. Never completed to McCartney's satisfaction, it remained unreleased until reactivated for this album. Recorded at home and overdubbed at Morgan Studios, the solo version is taken at a slightly faster tempo and benefits from a considered vocal arrangement.

'Maybe I'm Amazed' would have made a stunning debut single, but for some reason it was overlooked. "Sometimes we're a bit daft here," McCartney explained. "We have a bit of a funky organisation, you know, which isn't that clued into picking up tracks off albums. At the time we thought 'Maybe I'm Amazed' was a good track and maybe we should do that as a single, which it probably should have been. But we never did." Nonetheless, McCartney may have considered releasing the song as a single, because a promotional film by Charlie Jenkins was screened on British and American TV on April 19 1970.

When asked how he came to write the song, he said he couldn't particularly remember. "I know what it was about in my own mind, you know? It was about just getting married, I suppose, and just sort of saying, you know … the sort of doubt kind of thing of it all is what, I suppose, I was trying to sum up." He was obviously feeling troubled when he wrote 'Maybe I'm Amazed'. For much of 1969/70, he'd felt isolated, insecure, and worried; even his relationship with Linda, it appears, worried him. Yet it was Linda who shouldered the burden of his depression, hauling him out of his despondency by encouraging him to write. Although he found the music business disheartening, with Linda's help he turned to music as therapy. "It's worked for you before, you know," she is alleged to have told him.

A paean to self-realisation and Linda's indomitable spirit, 'Maybe I'm Amazed' finds McCartney exploring the deepest corners of his fragile psyche. It is an attempt at understanding his melancholia and coming to terms with it. If previously he appeared confident, even arrogant, privately McCartney was an emotional wreck. But at least he had an escape route that bypassed the usual slow descent into drink and drug abuse. 'Maybe I'm Amazed' is a song of deliverance and self-realisation. Even if McCartney felt he couldn't overcome his insecurities, at least he could recognise and write about them – and that was half the battle won.

'Maybe I'm Amazed' was completed in one productive session on February 22 1970 at Abbey Road. McCartney began the session with the intention of mixing 'That Would Be Something' and 'Valentine Day' to stereo. But he did that quicker than anticipated, so he remade 'Every Night' and then recorded 'Maybe I'm Amazed'. Its release as a single in 1977, seven years too late, meant that one of McCartney's finest songs failed to achieve the commercial success it deserved.

'Kreen-Akore' is an improvised instrumental recorded at Morgan Studios. McCartney was inspired by a television programme about the Kreen-Akrore Indians, who live in the Brazilian jungle. The documentary, *The Tribe That Hides From Man*, shown by ITV, revealed how the Indians' way of life was being altered by European settlers. With the programme fresh in his mind, he began work on the track. "The next day, after lunch, I did some drumming," he recalled. Improvising, McCartney added percussion, which included the unusual application of a guitar case, to simulate a stampede. He then overdubbed some heavily compressed breathing, which becomes increasingly frantic and oppressive as the tempo and textures develop. It's an unusual track, which manages to combine both melodic and rhythmic elements with startling effect, and his decision to programme the piece directly after 'Maybe I'm Amazed' was a daring, provocative way to close his first solo album.

### McCartney data
Apple issued the album with generic labels, with the title in a customised font, in a black paper inner sleeve and laminated gatefold sleeve. A striking abstract photograph by Linda graced the front cover, with a photograph of Paul and daughter Mary on the back. Gordon House and Roger Huggett designed the cover, which originally had a reversed gatefold sleeve – the record being placed in the front pocket rather than the rear. EMI manufactured copies of the album on the Parlophone label for export to European countries. The album was reissued in the mid 1970s with black and silver Capitol 'dome' labels and for a second time on April 2 1984 by EMI's FAME imprint (FA 413100-1) with generic Apple labels.

American pressings were issued with generic Apple labels with several variations. The first has the title, McCartney, and 'Paul McCartney' printed on separate lines, with song titles in two columns on the B-side label. The second has the title and 'Paul McCartney' on separate lines, and the song titles in one column on the B-side label. The third US label variation has the title and 'Paul McCartney' printed on separate lines, with 'MFD. BY CAPITOL RECORDS' etc and Capitol logo perimeter print on the B-side.

A fourth variation has the Apple label with only the title *McCartney*, in a custom font, and catalogue number SMAS-3363.

The gatefold sleeve was manufactured with three minor variations: with Apple's New York address on the back cover; with Apple's California address on the back cover; and with Apple's New York address and 'an abkco managed company' on the back cover. Capitol reissued *McCartney* with generic black and silver 'dome' labels in the mid 1970s. It was reissued by Columbia in the early 1980s with generic red labels (JC-36478, FC-36511, and PC-36478).

*McCartney* was issued on 8-track both in Britain (8X-PCS-7102) and the USA (8XT 3363). Columbia reissued the 8-track (JCA-36478) in the early 1980s. The album was also issued as a 7-inch reel-to-reel tape in the USA (Apple/Ampex L-3363) and in the UK (Apple/EMI TA-PMC 7102). The British reel-to-reel tape was in mono and remained on EMI's stock list until 1975.

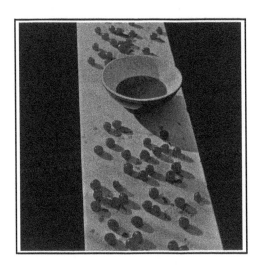

EMI export edition manufactured in the UK for sale in European countries.

EMI mid 70s re-issue

EMI mid 80s re-issue

18

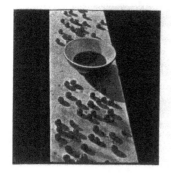

1971: Another Day to Wild Life

## 'ANOTHER DAY' / 'OH WOMAN, OH WHY'
## PAUL McCARTNEY
**UK release** February 19 1971; Apple R 5889; chart high No.2.
**US release** February 22 1971; Apple 1829; chart high No.5.

### 'Another Day' (Mr & Mrs McCartney)
Paul McCartney (vocals, guitar, bass), Linda McCartney (backing vocals), Dave Spinoza, Denny Seiwell (drums).
### 'Oh Woman, Oh Why' (McCartney)
Paul McCartney (vocals, bass), Linda McCartney (backing vocals), Hugh McCracken (guitars), Denny Seiwell (drums).
Both recorded at CBS Studios, New York City, NY, USA. Both mixed at A&R Studios, New York City, NY, USA. Both produced by Paul and Linda McCartney.

### 'ANOTHER DAY'
While John and Yoko were recovering from their primal therapy, Paul and Linda were busy recording their new album in New York City. 'Another Day' was recorded during the sessions for *Ram* but had been previewed two years earlier while filming *Let It Be*. Although it had been written speculatively for The Beatles, recorded solo it was a clear indication of the mature solo McCartney sound to come.

For the first time, the McCartneys' distinctive harmonies featured prominently. It was a deliberate attempt to create a unique McCartney style, a musical identity outside of The Beatles. "I wanted *our* sound," McCartney explained. "I wanted the amateur approach, something we could make ourselves and then work on. We've been writing many more songs and we're developing as a harmony team." Pushing for Linda to play a more active role in his career, he taught her to play keyboards and encouraged her as she had encouraged him a few months earlier. But his claim that she co-wrote 'Another Day' didn't wash with his publisher.

McCartney wasn't alone in wanting his wife to share songwriting credits and royalties: Lennon insisted that Ono had co-written some of his songs. As The Beatles' finances were in the hands of the official receivers, claims by McCartney and Lennon that their wives were contributing to their songs was little more than a ploy to double income from publishing. However, Sir Lew Grade, the new owner of Northern Songs, who published the Beatle catalogue, was having none of it.

McCartney told *Rolling Stone*: "Lew Grade suddenly saw his songwriting concessions – that he'd just paid an awful lot of money for, virtually to get hold of John and I – he suddenly saw that I was now claiming that I was writing half of my stuff with Linda, and that if I was writing half of it she was entitled to a pure half of it, no matter whether she was a recognised songwriter or not. I didn't think that that was important; I thought that whoever I worked with, no matter what the method of collaboration was, that person, if they did help me on the song, they should have a portion of the song for helping me."

The lawsuit was settled with McCartney agreeing to make a programme for Grade's television company. The embarrassment of *James Paul McCartney* aside, Grade's lawsuit had at least one positive outcome: it encouraged Linda to write. Her first attempt at song writing, 'Seaside Woman', was the result of pressure from both Grade and her husband. "I did a song, 'Seaside Woman', right after we'd been to Jamaica," she recalled. "That's when ATV was suing us saying I was incapable of writing, so Paul said, 'Get out and write a song.'"

Behind its glossy facade, 'Another Day' is an acute examination of isolation and social alienation. In one brief verse and chorus, McCartney records the sense of repetition that overshadows the daily routine of the suburbanite. His epistle to social estrangement documents a daily treadmill of tedium determined by economic interest and sexual compulsion and reveals the obsessive nature of fantasies that we engage in to obliterate time. The only escape is to hope and dream of the perfect lover, but even that's fleeting and ultimately frustrating. A song that maps the modern human condition, 'Another Day' comments on the loss of individualism and the way we vainly attemt to impose order on the chaotic reality of life.

Remarkably, it wasn't McCartney who selected 'Another Day' for release as a single but studio assistant Dixon Van Winkle. "We were sitting in Studio A2 one day listening to the takes and Paul asked me to pick the single," he recalled in *Mix*. "I had definite feelings about the record and was in love with 'Another Day'. Paul said, 'OK. 'Another Day' it is.' I mixed the track and David Crawford cut about 100 copies of it in a back room at A&R for the radio stations. The next day, when I heard it on the air, I realised it was a disaster. We got carried away with the bass part, and when it hit the radio station's compressor, it pumped like crazy. I learned that lesson real quick! But we never remixed the song, and Paul never said anything about it."

McCartney turns up the heat with 'Oh Woman, Oh Why', a tense, blusey rocker with a rip-roaring vocal. Economical basslines combine with Seiwell's thunderous drumming to establish a solid foundation upon which tight guitar lines interweave. McCartney's gritty vocal is one of his best and provides some raw and convincing authenticity to this blues-based rocker. Unusually for McCartney, 'Oh Woman, Oh Why' sees him questioning rather than celebrating womanhood. Rarely has he sounded so aggressive, which is particularly notable in light of the song's subject matter.

### 'Another Day' data
Apple issued 'Another Day' in Britain with generic Apple labels and a black paper sleeve. There were two label variants. Some copies have '*Joint interest claimed by McCartney Music Inc.' printed below the 'Northern Songs NCB' publishing credit; others have an additional claim '*Copyright also claimed by Maclen (Music) Ltd.' When the single was reissued in the mid 1970s with black and silver Capitol 'dome' labels, the publishing was claimed by 'McCartney Music by arrangement with ATV Music Ltd'. Demonstration copies were issued with a large 'A' at 2 o'clock and 'DEMO RECORD NOT FOR SALE' on three lines above the spindle hole.

Several label variations were produced in America. The first has a dark green Apple label; bold type with 'STEREO' at 10 o'clock; 'Recorded in England' at 8 o'clock; song title and artist name centre bottom; publisher information, catalogue number, and producer's name on the right of the label. The second variant has a dark green Apple label; song title and composer credits at 10 o'clock; 'STEREO' at 8 o'clock; artist name and 'Recorded in England' centre bottom. The third US label variant has a dark green Apple label; song title and composer credits at 11 o'clock on one line;

'STEREO' at nine o'clock; artist name and 'Recorded in England' centre bottom. The fourth has a light green Apple label; 'STEREO' at 9 o'clock; a black star at 8 o'clock; song title, songwriter, artist name, and 'Recorded in England' centre bottom. The fifth and last variant has a light green Apple label; song title and composer credits at 11 o'clock; 'STEREO' at 9 o'clock; artist name and 'Recorded in England' centre bottom.

Unique mono mixes of both A and B-side were produced for American AM radio stations and issued as a demonstration single (PRO-6193). Demonstration copies were issued with light green Apple labels with a black star, 'PROMOTIONAL RECORD' at 11 o'clock, and 'NOT FOR SALE' at 8 o'clock. The single was also issued in mono in France (2C006-04758M). Copies of the single manufactured in America with black and sliver Capitol 'dome' labels have 'Manufactured By MPL Communications, Inc.' added to the label perimeter text.

28

*RAM*
**PAUL AND LINDA McCARTNEY**
Side 1 'Too Many People', '3 Legs', 'Ram On', 'Dear Boy', 'Uncle Albert/Admiral Halsey', 'Smile Away'.
Side 2 'Heart Of The Country', 'Monkberry Moon Delight', 'Eat At Home', 'Long Haired Lady', 'Ram On', 'The Back Seat Of My Car'.
**UK release** May 21 1971; LP Apple PAS 10003; 8-track cartridge Apple 8X-PAS 10003; chart high No.1.
**US release** May 17 1971; LP Apple SMAS-3375; 8-track cartridge Apple 8XW3375; chart high No.2.

**'Too Many People' (McCartney)**
Paul McCartney (vocals, bass), Linda McCartney (backing vocals), Hugh McCracken (guitars), Denny Seiwell (drums).
**'3 Legs' (McCartney)**
Paul McCartney (vocals, bass), Linda McCartney (backing vocals), Dave Spinoza (guitars), Denny Seiwell (drums).
**'Ram On' (McCartney)**
Paul McCartney (piano, keyboards, ukulele, vocals), Linda McCartney (backing vocals).
**'Dear Boy' (Paul and Linda McCartney)**
Paul McCartney (vocals, bass, piano), Linda McCartney (backing vocals), Denny Seiwell (drums).
**'Uncle Albert/Admiral Halsey' (Paul and Linda McCartney)**
Paul McCartney (vocals, bass), Linda McCartney (backing vocals), Hugh McCracken (guitars), Denny Seiwell (drums), Marvin Stamm (trumpet), The New York Philharmonic Orchestra.
**'Smile Away' (McCartney)**
Paul McCartney (vocals, keyboards, bass), Linda McCartney (backing vocals), Hugh McCracken (guitars), Denny Seiwell (drums).
**'Heart Of The Country' (Paul and Linda McCartney)**
Paul McCartney (vocals, bass, guitar), Linda McCartney (backing vocals), Hugh McCracken (guitars), Denny Seiwell (drums).
**'Monkberry Moon Delight' (Paul and Linda McCartney)**
Paul McCartney (vocals, piano, bass), Linda McCartney (backing vocals), Hugh McCracken (guitars), Denny Seiwell (drums).
**'Eat At Home' (Paul and Linda McCartney)**
Paul McCartney (vocals, bass), Linda McCartney (backing vocals), Dave Spinoza (guitars), Denny Seiwell (drums).
**'Long Haired Lady' (McCartney)**
Paul McCartney (vocals, keyboards, bass), Linda McCartney (backing vocals), Hugh McCracken (guitars), Denny Seiwell (drums), The New York Philharmonic Orchestra.
**'The Back Seat Of My Car' (McCartney)**
Paul McCartney (vocals, piano, bass), Linda McCartney (backing vocals), Hugh McCracken (guitars), Denny Seiwell (drums), The New York Philharmonic Orchestra.
All recorded at Columbia Studios, New York City, NY, USA, except 'Uncle Albert / Admiral Halsey', 'Long Haired Lady', and 'The Back Seat Of My Car' recorded at Columbia Studios (tracking) and A&R Studios (orchestra), New York City, NY, USA. All mixed at Sound Recorders, Los Angeles, CA, USA. All produced by Paul and Linda McCartney.

## RAM

Although Lennon and McCartney may have considered themselves polar opposites, they were more alike than either might have cared to admit. Like John and Yoko, Paul and Linda had withdrawn from the public gaze, moving into a small, ramshackle cottage on the west coast of Scotland. His move not only marking a break with cosmopolitanism, but also temporary escape from Apple and The Beatles. Rejecting bachelorhood and the big city lifestyle, McCartney turned to writing about his experiences and the simple pleasures he found there.

So great was the pressure on McCartney that he suffered a mental breakdown. "I was going through a bad time, what I suspect was almost a nervous breakdown," he recalled. "I remember lying awake at nights shaking, which has not happened to me since. I had so much in me that I couldn't express, and it was just very nervy times, very difficult."

Like Lennon, McCartney wrote about his experiences and feelings. His songs from this time reflect both the pleasure and pain he experienced in the months after the Beatles split. They also express a growing discontentment with his former bandmates and in particular John Lennon.

Lennon and McCartney had been sniping at one another for months. The music press was full of their petulant squabbling and inevitably this found its way into their songs and albums. The early 1970s found all four Beatles using their songwriting skills to comment on the others. Ringo recorded 'Back Off Boogaloo', a song apparently attacking McCartney, and George included 'Sue Me Sue You Blues', a wry comment on The Beatles' business troubles, on his *Living In The Material World* album. Along with Lennon's *Imagine* album ('How Do You Sleep?' was a barbed critique of McCartney), *Ram* marked a low point in the ex-Beatles' relationship. Voicing their feelings in public was not the best way to manage the situation. Although it provided some kind of therapy, it was far from curative.

McCartney was in a bullish mood (or should that be ramish?). He was intent on telling his side of the story, and nobody was going to stop him. For him, the album's title, *Ram*, summarised exactly how he felt. "Ram seemed like a good word," he explained, "cos it not only meant ram forward, press on, be positive, that aspect of it. I also, as a lot of people probably know, am well into sheep, and have been for a number of years," he laughed, "since I got my Scottish farm and inherited a flock. So the ram being the male sheep was kind of good and sort of male and that kind of stuff."

To showcase his new approach, McCartney issued 'Another Day' as a standalone single. While this found favour with the public, the album received less than favourable reviews from the critics. Of the ex-Beatles, they preferred Lennon's raw primitivism to McCartney's urbane pop. Only months before McCartney released *Ram*, Lennon issued his *Plastic Ono Band* album and 'Power To The People' single, both of which offered intense, gutsy rock'n'roll. McCartney's welcoming pop, described by one critic as "suburban rock'n'roll", was the antithesis of Lennon's intense, angst-ridden primitivism.

McCartney characteristically shrugged off negative criticism, saying: "I still read the notices and stuff and they're usually bum ones when you're expecting them to be great. Like after *Ram*." Not every review was negative. Lon Goddard, writing in *Record Mirror*, gave the album a favourable notice and suggested that Paul and Linda's harmonies were on a par with those of The Everly Brothers.

Although Linda had contributed to the *McCartney* album, *Ram* was her baptism of fire. "God, I tell you I worked her on the album," McCartney recalled. "Because she hadn't done an awful lot, so it was a little bit out of tune. I was not too pleasant to live with, I suppose, then. She was all right; she took it. She understood that it had to be good and you couldn't let any shit through. I gave her a hard time, I must say, but we were pleased with the results; it just meant we really forced it. [We] worked on all the harmonies even if they were hard harmonies – just stuck on it. Elton John later said somewhere that he thought it was the best harmonies he'd heard in a long while."

Dixon Van Winkle, who worked on the *Ram* sessions as a studio assistant, recalled how the pair worked on their harmonies. "The interplay between Paul and Linda was sweet, especially when they were on-mic. Linda actually came up with some parts on her own – the entire backing vocals on 'Uncle Albert/Admiral Halsey' consists of the two of them – but when she needed a hand, Paul was great with her."

Linda's reward for all her hard work was equal billing – the record was credited to Paul And Linda McCartney. She also received co-author credits for several songs. As McCartney explained: "Linda and I have been writing songs together – and my publishers are suing because they don't believe she wrote them with me. You know: suddenly she marries him and suddenly she's writing songs. 'Oh, sure (wink, wink). Oh, sure, she's writing songs.'"

While Sir Lew Grade saw this as an infringement of his agreement with McCartney, George Martin thought Linda's influence was adversely affecting Paul's writing. "I don't think Linda is any substitute for John Lennon," he remarked. Obviously, Linda couldn't compete with Lennon as a writer, musician, or collaborator. Nevertheless, she fulfilled the key roles of performer and muse. But whether this justified a co-author credit is questionable.

Paul, Linda, and family few to New York City on January 3 1971 to begin work on the album. Auditions began two days later in one of the less glamorous parts of Manhattan. Everyone, no matter what their reputation, was up for audition. Guitarist Dave Spinoza was apparently none too pleased at having to audition; his reputation as one of New York's top session players was normally enough to secure any job. However, McCartney was taking no chances, and reputation alone was not enough. "You know a lot of other drummers were a bit put off by the idea of having to audition for Paul," Denny Seiwell explained. "I didn't mind at all and I went along to a really run down basement and just played for Paul and Linda. They liked it so I was in the band."

Spinoza's relationship with the McCartneys never really jelled and after working on '3 Legs' and several other songs, he quit the sessions. A hard-nosed New York session player, he wasn't prepared to jeopardise future sessions for McCartney. "I told them I couldn't keep every week open because when Paul got back to England there are other people that are going to keep me eating. I said I could make two of the days, but not five and Linda got very indignant." McCartney wasn't impressed with Spinoza's attitude and had McCracken finish the album.

Recording began on January 10 1971 with McCartney quickly establishing a professional, workmanlike atmosphere. According to David Spinoza, he instigated a regime of set hours. "In the studio, he's very businesslike. He came in at nine every morning. We'd listen to what we'd done the day before, then it was eight hours of just playing." Keeping to this routine, the group reportedly recorded 21 songs between January and March 1971. Of those, two were released as a standalone single ('Another Day' / 'Oh Woman Oh Why'), 12 featured on *Ram*, and two would appear on *Red Rose Speedway* ('Get On The Right Thing' and 'Little Lamb Dragonfly'). 'Little Woman Love' appeared as the B-side of 'Mary Had A Little Lamb', 'A Love For You' was issued on the *In-Laws* soundtrack, while 'Sunshine Sometime', 'Rode All Night', and 'Hey Diddle' were eventually issued on the deluxe edition of *Ram* issued on 21 May 2012.

Basic tracks were recorded as a three-piece with McCartney usually playing piano, Seiwell drums, and Spinoza or McCracken on guitar. Guitarist Spinoza recalled how the songs developed in the studio. "We both played acoustic and sometimes Paul played piano but never played bass while we were there. He overdubbed the bass later. It was a bit weird, because bass, drums, and guitar would have been more comfortable." McCartney overdubbed additional instrumentation on to the basic track before adding his and Linda's vocals. After recording at A&R Studios, where the bulk of the album was made, they moved to Columbia Studios, also in New York, to add additional overdubs, mainly the orchestral parts. Final mixing and programming was completed in Los Angeles at Sound Recorders.

### Ram songs

The album begins with two words directed at John Lennon: "Piss off." McCartney explained: "Yeah. Piss off, cake. Like, a piece of cake becomes piss off cake, and it's nothing, it's so harmless really, just little digs." His tirade didn't go unnoticed and, unsurprisingly, Lennon took 'Too Many People' personally. Although some suggested that this was just another case of Lennon's paranoia – he had good reasons to be paranoid – one look at the song's first verse confirms his suspicions.

McCartney later admitted that his lyric, every bit as vitriolic as Lennon's later 'How Do You Sleep?', was indeed aimed at his former partner. "I remember there was one little reference to John in the whole thing," he explained. "He'd been doing a lot of preaching, and it got up my nose a little bit. I wrote 'Too many people preaching practices' I think is the line. I mean, that was a little dig at John and Yoko. There wasn't anything else on it that was about them. Oh, there was 'Yoko took your lucky break and broke it in two.'"

More than a "little dig", this was McCartney at his most acerbic. Thankfully, he had the good sense to alter his original reference to Yoko, otherwise he may never have spoken with Lennon ever again. Lennon replied in kind. His *Imagine* album would include the cutting 'How Do You Sleep?' and a postcard depicting him grappling with a pig – a parody of the *Ram* cover.

Next up comes '3 Legs', a song loaded with ambiguous metaphors, which could be read as a commentary on the break-up of The Beatles and a thinly veiled critique of Lennon, Harrison and Starr. While McCartney's lyric seems to address his feelings about The Beatles' fall from grace, it also alludes to freedom and redemption, which he'd found in the wilds of Scotland. Like much of what he'd written for *Ram*, it finds him concealing his innermost feelings in metaphors and encrypted symbolism.

In 'Ram On', McCartney reflects on the here and now and suggests that he/we should live for the moment. Discarding the florid piano introduction in favour of a simple strummed ukulele, recalling simpler and perhaps more idyllic times, his arrangement reinforces the lyrical theme by rejecting flamboyance in favour of a simpler musical setting that mirrored his own back to basics approach to life. 'Ram On' fades midway and returns on side 2, thereby establishing what would become a long-standing practice for McCartney of bookending albums with a reprised musical theme to create an impression of continuity.

At the time, some read 'Dear Boy' as yet another critique of Lennon, and at first glance the lyric appears to confirm this. But McCartney later said: "'Dear Boy' wasn't getting at John, [it] was actually a song to Linda's ex-husband: 'I guess you never knew what you had missed.' I never told him that, which was lucky because he's since committed suicide. And it was a comment about him, cos I did think, 'Gosh, you know, she's so amazing, I suppose you didn't get it.'"

'Dear Boy' is, of course, as much about Paul and Linda as it is about her ex-husband, and in its own way it's as autobiographically revealing as McCartney gets. As with several songs from the earlier McCartney, 'Dear Boy' reveals that, post-Beatles, McCartney's mental well-being remained fragile and that it was only Linda's stabilising presence that pulled him from the abyss of despair.

Turning to his family for inspiration, McCartney called on his Uncle Albert, a colourful relation who, he recalled, "used to quote the Bible to everyone when he got drunk". 'Uncle Albert/Admiral Halsey' was fashioned from several unfinished tunes – the song has 12 distinct motifs – that were combined to complete the song. McCartney was well versed in this practice and often fused unfinished fragments when unable to complete a composition. He had taken this to its logical conclusion when various unfinished songs were brought together to form the 'long medley' on Abbey Road. Like the 'long medley', 'Uncle Albert/Admiral Halsey' has enough melodic twists and turns to keep the listener engaged, and the restrained use of the New York Philharmonic Orchestra, arranged by George Martin, further enhances the song's Beatle-esque qualities.

'Uncle Albert/Admiral Halsey' was cut in Studio B at CBS Studios on East 52nd Street in Manhattan, with CBS staff engineer Tim Geelan at the desk. "Working on 'Uncle Albert/Admiral Halsey' was one of the highlights of my career," says Geelan, "Paul was a great producer: thorough, businesslike and loose at the same time. They were very comfortable sessions that followed a pattern. We'd start working at nine or 10 in the morning. Paul would show Denny Seiwell, the drummer, and David Spinozza and Hugh McCracken, the guitar players who split the date, the song we'd be tracking that day. After rehearsing for several hours, we'd cut a version of the tune and then have a lunch break. After lunch, we'd listen to what we had and then record another couple of takes if it was necessary."

Guitarist Hugh McCracken had recorded several songs with McCartney, always under his direct supervision. However, when he came to record the basic tracks for 'Uncle Albert/Admiral Halsey', McCartney let the guitarist write his own parts. "This song represented a breakthrough in our musical relationship," McCracken recalled in Mix.

Mexican EP

Swedish 45

British reissue LP

"Paul is a genius. He sees and hears everything he wants, and would give specific instructions to me and the drummer. But he didn't know what he wanted the guitar part to be like on this song. I asked him to trust me, and he did. After I came up with the parts, he was very pleased. For the rest of the record, Paul let me try things out before making any suggestions."

In 'Smile Away' McCartney examines the apparent hypocrisy of his adversaries (Klein and the other ex-Beatles) and finds them wanting. While each would claim otherwise, the McCartney-Lennon nexus was stronger than either of them cared to admit. When it came to slagging one another off, each expressed himself in remarkably similar ways. McCartney often attempted to conceal this side of his personality, but 'Smile Away', like Lennon's 'How Do You Sleep?', reveals that he was as capable of vitriol as his former partner.

'Heart Of The Country' finds McCartney re-examining the symbolic divide between town and country, a subject he had explored before in 'Mother Nature's Son'. The notion of getting back to the country in order to 'get it together' was adopted by many musicians in the late 1960s and early 1970s. The Beatles, who could afford it more than most, became increasingly aware of the need to escape the pressures of fame, and they sought fulfilment through spiritual rather than material means.

Presented in a breezy country style, 'Heart Of The Country' adumbrates McCartney's belief in that notion. A mini manifesto, it documents the changes and benefits to his mental and physical wellbeing brought forth by a bucolic lifestyle. Delighting in his new-found facility, McCartney employs a jazz-styled bridge, complete with scat singing, to drive the point home.

He was motivated to write 'Monkberry Moon Delight' through a fascination with his children's malapropisms and a fondness for the songsmiths Leiber and Stoller. As he explained: "When my kids were young they used to call milk 'monk' for whatever reason that kids do – I think it's magical the way that kids can develop better names for things than the real ones. In fact, as a joke, Linda and I still occasionally refer to an object by that child-language name. So, monk was always milk, and monkberry moon delight was a fantasy drink, rather like 'Love Potion No. 9,' hence the line in the song 'sipping monkberry moon delight.' It was a fantasy milk shake."

It's a light-hearted romp of a song, full of surreal imagery, its antecedents lying in The Beatles' delight with chance and instantaneity. From the mid 1960s, Lennon and McCartney's lyrics began to read like surrealist poetry. Jumbled allusions to sensory experiences ('Strawberry Fields Forever') and multiple self-referencing ('Glass Onion') crept into their songs. Like the Surrealists before them, they delighted in playing games to generate random juxtapositions ('Hello, Goodbye'), which they would use to leap from one idea to another.

'Monkberry Moon Delight' was written in the same spontaneous way. McCartney used his children's words as a springboard for free association. Look for meaning if you wish, but his lyric was intended to confuse. His imagery defies logic; confused and absurd, it is pure automatism. The Beatles knew that almost everything they wrote would be analysed until every last drop of meaning had been squeezed from it. The cross-referencing they fed into their lyrics was a game they played to see how much meaning could be read into something that resulted from chance. McCartney replays that game here, with obvious delight.

Speaking to *Rolling Stone* magazine in early 1970, McCartney made it clear where his interests lay. "For me life at home is what interests me now. I have two kids, a wife of one year and everything at home. I love being at home and I love music." Searching for inspiration, McCartney combined the two and wrote about the delights of Linda's home cooking – he'd return to the subject again for 'Cook Of The House'. As substantial as one of Linda's vegetarian casseroles, 'Eat At Home' finds its author once again extolling the virtues of domestic bliss and, of course, the love of a good woman. Influenced by his hero, Buddy Holly, McCartney's upbeat slice of retro-pop was so popular in some territories that it was issued as a single.

'Long Haired Lady' was written as a tribute to Linda but fails to match earlier love songs dedicated to her. When Lennon wrote about Yoko or Harrison about Patti, both managed to avoid the overt sentimentality of McCartney's heartfelt but insipid lyric. If the best he could do was to describe Linda as his "sweet little lass" (patronising) or "long haired lady" (superficial), then George Martin was right: Paul's songwriting could be uninspired.

'The Back Seat Of My Car' may have been intended for *Abbey Road* as it was one of several new compositions that McCartney previewed while filming *Let It Be* at Twickenham Studios. However, like many songs presented at this time, it was held back for a solo project. McCartney's early readings of the song were peppered with jokey allusions to The Beach Boys, which he developed while recording the song in New York. A homage to the fictionalised fantasy America of his youth, 'The Back Seat Of My Car' is an idealised expression of teenage love: its visual counterpart is the squeaky-clean, formulaic, romantic comedies that populated 1950s cinema.

Explaining the song, he said: "'The Back Seat Of My Car' is the ultimate teenage song, and even though it was a long time since I was a teenager and had to go to a girl's dad and explain myself, it's that kind of meet-the-parents song. It's a good old driving song. And obviously 'back seat' is snogging, making love." However, unlike the lightweight films to which it alludes, 'The Back Seat Of My Car' has substance and weight. A song on a grand, elegant scale, its sweeping range gives it a celebratory feel. Its repeated refrain, "We believe that we can't be wrong", supports its upbeat theme. Unsurprisingly Lennon read it as another personal insult. His reply was typical. "Well," he said, "I believe that you could just be wrong." Although it had little to do with their feuding, that Lennon could read it as such says much about the state of their relationship at the time.

## Ram data

In Britain, *Ram* was issued by Apple with generic labels, in a laminated gatefold sleeve designed by McCartney. (Early editions are laminated inside and out, later editions are only laminated outside.) American pressings were issued with light or dark green Apple labels in three variations: credited to 'Paul and Linda McCartney', Apple label with small Capitol logo within perimeter print on B-side; credited to 'Paul and Linda McCartney', Apple label with 'MFD BY APPLE RECORD INC' perimeter print on B-side; or unsliced Apple B-side labels on both sides of the record.

The LP was reissued in the mid 1970s with black and silver Capitol 'dome' labels, in Britain and America. In the early 1980s, Columbia reissued the LP (JC-36479 and PC-36479).

Apple/Capitol issued *Ram* on 8-track in Britain (8X-PAS 10003) and the USA (8XW 3375). When Columbia obtained the rights to McCartney's back catalogue in the 1980s it reissued the 8-track (JCA 36479). Apple/Ampex issued *Ram* in America as a stereo 7-inch reel-to-reel tape (L-3375).

EMI issued the album on CD in Britain on its Capitol imprint on April 25 1987 and issued a remastered edition (CDPMCOL2) on July 7 1993. In America, Capitol issued the CD (CDP 7 46612 2) on January 17 1988 and DCC Compact Classics issued a gold CD (GZS-1037) in 1993.

To promote *Ram*, Apple issued mono pressings of the LP (MAS-3375) to American radio stations. The promotional album was mastered from an alternative mono mix of the album. (The LP was issued in mono in Brazil, although this was more probably a simple mono reduction of the stereo master rather than the McCartney-sanctioned mono mix used for the American promo LP.) The mono mix was eventually issued on CD as part of the 2012 deluxe reissue of *Ram*, and as a limited, numbered vinyl edition.

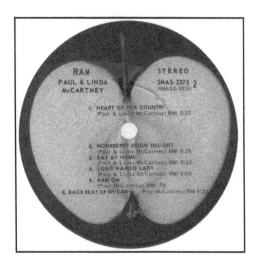

*BRUNG TO EWE BY*
PAUL AND LINDA McCARTNEY
**US release** Apple 12-inch promotional record SPRO-6210.

**'Now Hear This Song Of Mine'**
Various personnel. Recorded at A&R Studios and Columbia Studios, New York City, NY, USA, and Sound Recorders, Los Angeles, CA, USA. Produced by Paul and Linda McCartney.

BRUNG TO EWE BY
While working on *Ram*, Paul and Linda recorded 'Now Hear This Song Of Mine', an extended jingle designed to promote the album. Fifteen versions of the song, ranging in length from 30 seconds to just over a minute, were issued on a 12-inch promotional record. Unlike Britain, which at the time had only one national radio station playing rock music, the USA had hundreds, all clamouring for exclusive material. It would have been impossible for the McCartneys to visit them all, so issuing a promotional record distributed through MPL's New York office got round the problem of supply and demand.

*Brung To Ewe By* **data**
The 12-inch one-sided record (SPRO 6210), titled *Brung To Ewe By*, was issued either in the commercial *Ram* LP cover or in a plain white sleeve. It was accompanied by two letters, one from Paul and Linda, the other from their production company. Original copies of the disc were banded evenly and each song 'paused' at the end for radio convenience. Counterfeit copies were manufactured with uneven banding and played straight through (and some were pressed on coloured vinyl).

## 'UNCLE ALBERT / ADMIRAL HALSEY' / 'TOO MANY PEOPLE'
## PAUL AND LINDA McCARTNEY
**US release** August 2 1971; Apple 1837; chart high No.1.

### 'UNCLE ALBERT'
Issued by Apple as a single in the USA, 'Uncle Albert/Admiral Halsey' went to number 1 on all the major singles charts. Issued with generic Apple labels and a black paper sleeve, the single was manufactured with six label variations.

Variant one has a light green Apple label; bold type with 'STEREO' at 9 o'clock; song title and writer's credit at 10 o'clock; artist's name and 'Copyright also claimed by McCartney Music, Inc,- BMI' centre bottom. Variant two has a medium green Apple label; bold type with 'STEREO' at 1 o'clock; song title and writer's credit at 10 o'clock; 'Copyright also claimed by McCartney Music, Inc, BMI' at 8 o'clock; artist's name centre bottom. Variant three has a dark green Apple label; plain type with 'STEREO' at 9 o'clock; song title and writer's credit at 10 o'clock; artist's name and 'Copyright also claimed by McCartney Music, Inc,- BMI' centre bottom. Variant four is as three but with a full dark green Apple A-side label on both sides. Variant five has a dark green Apple label; bold type with 'STEREO' at 9 o'clock; song title top centre; writer's credit at 10 o'clock; 'Copyright also claimed by McCartney Music, Inc,- BMI' at 8 o'clock; artist's name centre bottom. Variant six is as five but with a full dark green Apple A-side label on both sides.

Demonstration copies of the single (PRO-6279) were manufactured with mono mixes of the A and B-side. The single was reissued in the mid 1970s with black and silver Capitol 'dome' labels.

## 'THE BACK SEAT OF MY CAR' / 'HEART OF THE COUNTRY'
## PAUL AND LINDA McCARTNEY
**UK release** August 13 1971; Apple R 5914; chart high No.39.

### 'THE BACK SEAT OF MY CAR'
Released as a single in Britain rather than 'Uncle Albert/Admiral Halsey', 'The Back Seat Of My Car' failed to match the commercial success of its US counterpart, barely making it into the Top 40. The single may have suffered from the restructuring then taking place at Apple Records. After Allen Klein moved back to New York City, the British side of the business all but ceased trading. By the time 'The Back Seat Of My Car' came out, most of Apple's releases were being co-ordinated through the company's American office.

### 'The Back Seat Of My Car' data
Issued with generic Apple labels and paper sleeve, this release was exclusive to Britain: most of Europe went with 'Eat At Home'. Apple issued demonstration copies with a large 'A' at 10 o'clock and 'DEMO RECORD NOT FOR SALE' on three lines above the spindle hole. The single was issued in the mid 1970s with black and silver Capitol 'dome' labels. Publishing credits for the B-side, 'Heart Of The Country', were changed from 'Northern Songs NCB Copyright also claimed by McCartney Music Inc' to 'McCartney Music Ltd by arrangement with ATV Music Ltd.'

Decca contract pressing. Note different text layout.

**WILD LIFE**
WINGS
**Side 1** 'Mumbo', 'Bip Bop', 'Love Is Strange', 'Wild Life'.
**Side 2** 'Some People Never Know', 'I Am Your Singer', 'Bip Bop Link', 'Tomorrow', 'Dear Friend', 'Mumbo Link'.
**UK release** November 15 1971; LP Apple PCS 7142; 8-track cartridge Apple 8X-PCS 7142 released January 1972; chart high No.8.
**US release** December 6 1971; LP Apple SW-3386; 8-track cartridge Apple 8XW 3386; chart high No.10.

**'Mumbo' (Paul and Linda McCartney)**
Paul McCartney (vocals, bass), Linda McCartney (keyboards, backing vocals), Denny Laine (guitar), Denny Seiwell (drums).
**'Bip Bop' (Paul and Linda McCartney)**
Paul McCartney (vocals, bass), Linda McCartney (backing vocals), Denny Laine (guitar), Denny Seiwell (drums).
**'Love Is Strange' (Smith, Baker)**
Paul McCartney (vocals, bass), Linda McCartney (keyboards, backing vocals), Denny Laine (guitar), Denny Seiwell (drums).
**'Wild Life' (Paul and Linda McCartney)**
Paul McCartney (vocals, bass), Linda McCartney (keyboards, backing vocals), Denny Laine (guitar), Denny Seiwell (drums).
**'Some People Never Know' (Paul and Linda McCartney)**
Paul McCartney (vocals, piano), Linda McCartney (backing vocals), Denny Laine (guitar), Denny Seiwell (drums).
**'I Am Your Singer' (Paul and Linda Mc-Cartney)**

Paul McCartney (vocals, bass), Linda McCartney (vocals), Denny Laine (guitar), Denny Seiwell (drums), Carl Dolmetsch Family (recorders).
**'Bip Bop Link' (Paul and Linda McCartney)**
Paul McCartney (guitar).
**'Tomorrow' (Paul and Linda McCartney)**
Paul McCartney (vocals, piano), Linda McCartney (backing vocals), Denny Laine (guitar), Denny Seiwell (drums).
**'Dear Friend' (Paul and Linda McCartney)**
Paul McCartney (vocals, piano), Linda McCartney (backing vocals), Denny Seiwell (drums).
**'Mumbo Link' (Paul and Linda McCartney)**
Paul McCartney (vocals, bass), Denny Laine (guitar), Denny Seiwell (drums).
All recorded at Abbey Road Studios, London, England. All produced by Paul and Linda McCartney.

WILD LIFE

Musically, *Wild Life* is to McCartney as *Plastic Ono Band* is to Lennon. But where the bite of Lennon's *Plastic Ono Band* resulted from a desire to express the pain of primal scream, the coarseness of *Wild Life* resulted from expedience. McCartney was eager to work with a band and, in line with the on-off back-to-basics philosophy he'd adopted since leaving The Beatles, he wanted to keep it simple. Keen to get back on the road, he assembled a new band. Starting from scratch, he acquired drummer Denny Seiwell, who had worked on *Ram*, and guitarist Denny Laine, late of The Moody Blues. Guitarist Hugh McCracken was asked to join but, although he attended rehearsals, he decided against joining the group.

This as-yet unnamed band rehearsed at Rude Studio (a small 4-track demo studio in a wood-lined, stone-walled building on McCartney's farm in Scotland). "I rang Denny Laine asking him to join us and we rehearsed for one or two days," McCartney explained. "I think, I showed him the chords and we went straight into the studio for the next three days doing all the backing tracks and within two weeks it [the album] was finished."

Pleased with their first sessions, McCartney introduced his new band to the press on August 3 1971. He'd toyed with various names for the band before settling on Wings. "We were thinking of all sorts of names, we had a new group and we had to think of a new name," he said. "We had a letter from an old gentleman in Scotland which said, 'Dear Paul, I see you are looking for a name for your group. I'd like to suggest "The Dazzlers"! So we were nearly The Dazzlers you know, with the big sequined jackets – still might be. But we thought no, something a little more earthy, so we thought of Turpentine…" McCartney eventually found the right name on September 13 while Linda was giving birth to their third daughter, Stella. Complications with the birth meant that Stella was born by Caesarean section, which ensured that McCartney was not present when his daughter entered the world. Ushered into a waiting room, he thought of the name Wings. "I sat next door in my green apron praying like mad … [and] the name Wings came into my head," he recalled.

Explaining his reason for recording the album so quickly, McCartney said: "I was inspired by Dylan, the way he just comes in the studio and everyone just falls in and makes a track." Like the *McCartney* album before it, some of the songs were 'made up' on the spot. Production was kept simple and five of the eight tracks were apparently first takes. *Wild Life* was a valiant attempt to capture the moments of magical spontaneity that McCartney finds so rewarding. Unfortunately, the 'magic' he was hoping for simply never materialised. Nevertheless, *Wild Life* captured a moment of becoming that was both brave and startlingly honest. Intended as a beginning, it made public what most bands do in private – but most people just weren't ready for this kind of unabashed openness, at least not from McCartney.

Promoted with a party at the Mecca Ballroom on London's Leicester Square on November 8 1971, *Wild Life* had a lot to live up to. Expectations were high and comparisons inevitable, but when styli began hitting plastic, there was a shock. Savaged by the critics, the album nevertheless has much to offer. Although some of the songs are obvious throwaways, it has several McCartney compositions that are as good as anything he's written. *Wild Life* is a breath of fresh air: crude, uncomplicated, and often wanting, it nevertheless has bags of character.

## Wild Life songs

'Mumbo' opens the album and was written while jamming with the band. Little more than a throwaway, its raw energy more than makes up for what it lacks in lyrical content (most of the lyrics are incomprehensible, so perhaps McCartney should have called it 'Mumble'). It's almost as if McCartney is unable to define or express the pent-up feelings he was still coming to terms with. Perhaps they were too intense to be expressed rationally, so he resorts to pure emotion to convey how he was feeling.

There was another reason for writing like this: it provided material quickly, and Wings desperately needed new material. It also gave McCartney the opportunity to check out the band and promote a sense of collective purpose through group participation. Proof that Wings were working at lightning speed can be heard in McCartney's opening remarks. Addressed to engineer Tony Clarke – best known for his work with The Moody Blues – "Take it, Tony" was intended to ensure that Clarke captured the song on tape. McCartney later admitted: "I think, in fact, [that] often we never gave the engineer a chance to even set up a balance."

A mid-tempo rocker, 'Bip Bop', follows, and while this has the advantage of proper lyrics, it still falls short of what McCartney was capable of. The author himself wasn't impressed with his efforts, saying: "It just goes nowhere; I still cringe every time I hear it." Could this really have been composed by the same person who a few years previously had written a string of urbane, considered, intelligent pop songs? Unfortunately, the answer is yes.

'Love Is Strange' had already proved successful for Mickey & Sylvia and later The Everly Brothers, providing them with a British hit in 1965. Before Wings began recording, Paul and Linda spent some time in Jamaica, where they enthusiastically investigated the local music scene. The couple returned home with a quantity of reggae singles, to which Linda added a copy of the recently released *Tighten Up* compilation, which she played incessantly.

By the early 1970s, the popularity of reggae had grown considerably. Jamaican musicians were not only recording hits, they were expanding musical perimeters and influencing European musicians. Inspired by what they heard, the McCartneys decided to record a reggae-influenced instrumental. "We were just playing it and it was great music," McCartney told Kid Jensen. "We just loved it so we started with a backing track we got the band together and just started to play the reggae thing. It's not as easy as you think you know, it's not easy at all. I suppose it is for Jamaicans but it's a whole other thing. Anyway, we did this backing track, and decided that 'Love Is Strange' would fit over it, so we started singing over it and that's how it ended up." McCartney gave the song a 'reggae' arrangement because, he explained, "reggae is the newest and best beat around. There are more possibilities with reggae than anything at the moment".

On the surface, 'Wild Life' appears to be a song about animal rights, and as such could mark the beginning of the McCartneys' long engagement with the cause. Certainly at this time, the McCartneys were beginning to embrace vegetarianism. But when John Mendelsohn reviewed the song for *Rolling Stone*, he suggested that it might be a subtle parody of Lennon's political engagement, bolstering his argument by pointing to McCartney's vocal, which at times hints at the kind of primal screaming that Lennon employed for much of his *Plastic Ono Band* album. If, as Mendelsohn suggests, 'Wild Life' criticises left-wing activism – and there are clues that this might be the case – then it's as astute a piece of political analysis as anything Lennon or any left-wing intellectual ever conceptualised. Of course, it could still just be a song about animal rights.

Dating from the summer of 1969, 'Some People Never Know' was written while the McCartneys holidayed in Barbados. A typically melodic ballad, it could easily have appeared on any of The Beatles' later albums and not sounded out of place. Resigned to the fact that others will never know what it means to love, McCartney uses music as a metaphor to explore his relationship with Linda. This may sound sentimental, but any gushiness is dispelled by the obvious tenderness of his lyric. Like much of the material on *Wild Life*, 'Some People Never Know' relies on understatement to underline meaning.

Songs obviously mean a lot to McCartney, so it made perfect sense to employ the concept as a metaphor for his relationship with Linda. 'I Am Your Singer' is sung as a duet as McCartney calls on the reciprocity of singer and song to represent their relationship. Each enhances the other and neither can work successfully on its own. This may sound like the kind of unbearably sentimental fetish that lovers indulge in, but any sentimentality is effectively effaced by a strong melody, an honest lyric, and simple but effective instrumentation that focuses attention on the vocal interaction between husband and wife. A sincere expression of requited love, its allusions to freedom and escape prefigure themes McCartney would explore on *Band On The Run*.

'I Am Your Singer' is followed by the first of two brief instrumentals. The first, 'Bip Bop Link', is a simple acoustic guitar doodle; the second, 'Mumbo Link', which comes at the end of the album, is a brief jam – probably recorded while studio engineers were balancing recording levels. Both were credited to the McCartneys, although the second sounds more like a spontaneous improvisation involving Seiwell and Laine – Linda doesn't appear to be involved. The two pieces were originally untitled and were only named when the album was released on CD.

'Tomorrow', another song about Paul and Linda's relationship, reveals how much things had changed. A year previously, McCartney had bemoaned his loss of confidence; even Linda couldn't draw him out of his melancholia. Now in buoyant mood, he expressed his rediscovered self-confidence with a bright, breezy melody that is uplifting and self-assured. Yet despite an equally optimistic lyric, it's obvious that he was still reliant on Linda for support. If 'I Am Your Singer' suggested emotional reciprocity, 'Tomorrow' hints at his fears of future rejection and his reliance on Linda to get him through his dark nights of the soul. If the McCartneys' world wasn't perfect, 'Tomorrow' suggests that at least their future looked rosy.

'Dear Friend' finds McCartney contemplating his relationship with Lennon. As subtle a piece of writing as he's produced, its sensitive lyrics and emotive melody evoke a sense of resignation that mirrored his feelings about his former partner. Long after Lennon's death, McCartney said: "'Dear Friend' was written about John, yes. I don't like grief and arguments, they always bug me. Life is too precious, although we often find ourselves guilty of doing it. So after John had slagged me off in public, I had to think of a response, and it was either going to be [to] slag him off in public – some instinct stopped me, which I'm really glad about – or do something else. So I worked on my attitude and wrote 'Dear Friend', saying, in effect, let's lay the guns down, let's hang up our boxing gloves." McCartney appears to have forgotten that he had spent some of *Ram*, not to mention what he said in the press, slagging off Lennon. However, 'Dear Friend' does point to a reconciliation, even if at the time both would have rejected the possibility as nonsense.

### *Wild Life* data

No singles were taken from the album either in Britain or in the USA, although a couple sneaked out in other countries. Odeon issued 'Wild Life', split into two parts, as a single in Venezuela (278 - A [YEX 871]). An edit of 'Love Is Strange' lasting 4:07 was scheduled for release as a single in Britain (Apple R 5932) and white label copies were manufactured with 'I Am Your Singer' on the B-side, but it never appeared. 'Love Is Strange' did appear on the B-side of 'Bip Bop' when it was issued by Apple as a single in Turkey (45-LA 4342) and Mexico issued a four-track EP (EPEM-10604) that featured 'Love Is Strange', 'I Am Your Singer', 'Tomorrow' and 'Mumbo'. The EP was issued in mono with generic Apple labels and picture sleeve.

The LP was issued with customised labels that feature photographs Paul and Linda had taken of one another, and a yellow paper inner sleeve. The cover, printed on thick card (an oblique reference to the rock'n'roll albums of McCartney's youth), was as uncompromising as the music. At a time when rock was becoming increasingly sophisticated and urbane, Wings positioned themselves as fervent ruralists diametrically opposed to the emergent glam rock scene then sweeping the country.

Because the cover did not feature the band's name or album title, in America Capitol placed a 4-inch by 2-inch rectangular sticker to the front cover with 'WINGS "WILD LIFE"' in yellow. A second white rectangular sticker with 'Paul McCartney and Friends' in blue was produced for later editions.

EMI re-released *Wild Life* in the mid 1980s on its budget FAME imprint (FA 416101-1) with generic black and silver Parlophone labels and a plain white inner sleeve. In America, Columbia reissued the album with generic red labels (FC-36480 and PC-36480).

The album was issued on 8-track cartridge in Britain (8X-PCS 7142) and America (8XW 3375). The American edition of the 8-track was issued without an Apple logo on the cover but with the text '© McCartney Productions, Inc 1971' printed below Apple's address. Columbia reissued the 8-track (JCA 36480) in the early 1980s.

EMI issued *Wild Life* on CD (CD-FA 3101) on its FAME imprint on October 5 1987 and reissued a remastered edition on Parlophone (CDPMCOL3) on June 20 1989. Capitol issued the CD (CDM 7 52017 2) on same day in 1989.

EMI mid-70s reissue.

1972: Give Ireland Back To The Irish to Hi, Hi, Hi

**'GIVE IRELAND BACK TO THE IRISH' / 'GIVE IRELAND BACK TO THE IRISH (VERSION)'**
**WINGS**
**UK release** February 25 1972; Apple R 5936; chart high No.16.
**US release** February 28 1972; Apple 1847; chart high No.21.

**'Give Ireland Back To The Irish' (McCartney, McCartney)**
**'Give Ireland Back To The Irish (Version)' (McCartney, McCartney)**
Both with Paul McCartney (vocals, bass, tin whistle), Linda McCartney (keyboards, backing vocals), Denny Laine (guitar and tin whistle), Henry McCullough (guitar), Denny Seiwell (drums). Both recorded at Abbey Road Studios and mixed at Island or Apple Studios, London, England. Both produced by The McCartneys.

'GIVE IRELAND BACK TO THE IRISH'
McCartney could hardly be accused of playing it safe with the release of this Wings debut single (the first by the Mk.2 line-up: Paul, Linda, Laine, and Seiwell, plus new guitarist Henry Mc-Cullough). It was also the first Wings release to feature Henry McCullough, an Irish guitarist who'd played with Eire Apparent and the Grease Band, but who was unknown to McCartney at the time. "When we began looking for a second guitarist, it was Denny Laine who suggested McCullough," recalled McCartney. "I'd never met Henry until the other day, we were talking about getting another guitarist into the group just to thicken it out a bit and Denny knew Henry so he said 'there's this fellow…' we said get him along to see how good he is. So he came along and he was very good."

Written in response to the Bloody Sunday Massacre that occurred in Northern Ireland on January 30 1972, 'Give Ireland Back To The Irish' was politically committed but naive. Where Lennon used the old trick of turning a cliché on its head to make a satirical comment ('The Luck Of The Irish' on *Sometime In New York City*), McCartney's appraisal of the situation was less successful. Speaking to *Sounds*, he said: "Our government happened to be shooting Irish people, and I thought that was real bad news, and I felt I had to say something about it. I'm glad I did because, looking back, I could have just sat through it and not have said anything. But it was just that it got so near home on that particular day I felt I had to say something."

Say something he did, but 'Give Ireland Back To The Irish' was little more than an exercise in venting anger and lacks much in the way of analysis. It may have assuaged McCartney's rage, but all it did was cause trouble for its author and his band.

UK sleeve

US sleeve

"I wrote 'Give Ireland Back To The Irish', we recorded it and I was promptly phoned by the Chairman of EMI, Sir Joseph Lockwood, explaining that they wouldn't release it. He thought it was too inflammatory. I told him that I felt strongly about it and they had to release it. He said, 'Well it'll be banned', and of course it was – the BBC couldn't not play it. It was just one of those things you have to do in life because you believe in the cause. And protest was the context of the times. I knew 'Give Ireland Back to the Irish' wasn't an easy route, but it just seemed to me to be the time. All of us in Wings felt the same about it. But Henry McCullough's brother who lived in Northern Ireland was beaten up because of it. The thugs found out that Henry was in Wings."

'Give Ireland Back To The Irish' was performed during Wings university tour a few weeks before it was released as a single. As McCartney knew the song would be banned, playing it live was the only way anybody was going to hear it. Perhaps this was another reason for Wings hitting the road in early '72. With only a handful of songs to choose from, it was regularly performed twice in the same set, and despite its shortcomings as a song, it went down very well with the student audiences.

If McCartney was hoping to promote the song, he would have been better advised to push the B-side to radio stations. An instrumental version emulating a practice of vocal/instrumental releases favoured by reggae bands, it's far more enjoyable than the lacklustre A-side. The addition of a folky guitar motif and tin whistles gives the track some much needed sparkle. Not available on CD, this version is available from iTunes.

'Give Ireland Back To The Irish' was still causing problems almost 30 years after its original release. When McCartney wanted to include it on *Wingspan – Hits And History*, EMI asked for it to be removed. "I support the idea of Ireland being free and being handed back," explained McCartney. "I feel that, like a lot of people; but I don't support [the IRA's] methods. I certainly don't want to be in support when a bomb goes off in London and people are killed. I would have a hard time supporting that. So when EMI rang me up and said, 'Look, you know, we're pretty nervous and you don't have much time on the album. We should pull that one,' that was really why it got pulled."

### 'Give Ireland Back To The Irish' data
The single was released with customised labels featuring five shamrocks (symbolic of the new five piece line-up?) in a generic yellow Wings sleeve.

British pressings exist with two label variations. Original pressings have 'Northern Songs Ltd' as the publisher, with 'Copyright also claimed by Kidney Punch Music'. The single was reissued in 1976, by which time the publishing credit had changed to 'McCartney Music Ltd by arrangement with ATV Music Ltd'. These pressings also include the legend 'EMI Records Ltd' printed below the band's name.

American singles were issued with the same label design as British pressings and in yellow Wings sleeves with the addition of the song's lyrics. Reissued in 1976, the single was manufactured with black and silver labels.

## 'MARY HAD A LITTLE LAMB' / 'LITTLE WOMAN LOVE'
## WINGS
**UK release** May 5 1972; Apple R 5949; chart high No.9.
**US release** May 29 1972; Apple 1851; chart high No.28.

### 'Mary Had A Little Lamb' (McCartney, McCartney)
Paul McCartney (vocals, piano), Linda McCartney (backing vocals), Heather and Mary McCartney (backing vocals), Denny Laine (bass), Henry McCullough (mandolin), Denny Seiwell (drums). Recorded at Olympic Sound Studios, Barnes, England. Produced by The McCartneys.
### 'Little Woman Love' (McCartney, McCartney)
Paul McCartney (vocals, piano, bass), Linda McCartney (backing vocals), Hugh McCracken (guitars), Denny Seiwell (drums). Recorded at CBS Studios, New York City, NY, USA. Produced by The McCartneys.

'MARY HAD A LITTLE LAMB'
While 'Give Ireland Back To The Irish' had been written out of frustration and revulsion, Wings' second single was inspired by the McCartneys' children. When asked why a nursery rhyme, McCartney said: "I'm a Gemini, and I know that one minute I might be doing 'Ireland' and the next I'll be doing 'Mary Had A Little Lamb'. I can see how that would look from the sidelines, but the thing is we're not either of those records, but we are both of them."

However, his attempt to negate categorisation failed to counteract suggestions that 'Mary Had A Little Lamb' was simply an expression of contempt aimed at the censors who'd banned his previous single, and its release did little to appease either critics or public, who were becoming disenchanted with his catholic taste.

As he explained it, his reasons for writing 'Mary Had A Little Lamb' were less involved and more prosaic. "Now, you know, I've just got three kids over the last few years, and when I am sitting at home playing at the piano my audience a lot of the time is the kids." His daughter Mary enjoyed hearing her name mentioned in song, so dad wrote one for her. Or rather he wrote a new melody to accompany an existing verse. "I just wrote that one up, the words were already written, you know? I just found out what the words to the nursery rhyme were, wrote a little tune up around it, [and] went and recorded it." He later admitted that the record might have disappointed fans. "I see now ... that it wasn't much of a record," he confessed. True, with no middle eight or solo, the song tends to drag, but its chorus is infuriatingly catchy.

'Little Woman Love', inspired by Linda, is a breezy rocker with a rolling piano lick that gives it a cute rockabilly feel. Recorded in New York City while the McCartneys worked on *Ram*, this typically slick McCartney recording wouldn't have sounded out of place on either *Ram* or *Red Rose Speedway*, which would feature another two outtakes from the *Ram* sessions.

Mary Had A Little Lamb

R.5949

Mary Had A Little Lamb
1851

Little Woman Love
1851

### 'Mary Had A Little Lamb' data

Apple issued 'Mary Had A Little Lamb' in Britain and the USA with customised labels and in a picture cover. In America, Capitol manufactured two variants of the picture cover: one with 'Little Woman Love' printed on it, the other without.

The record was reissued by EMI and Capitol in the mid 1970s with black and silver Capitol 'dome' labels and MPL production credits rather than an Apple Records credit. To promote the single in America, Capitol issued white-label demonstration copies with black text and the artist credit 'Paul McCartney'.

# Mary Had A Little Lamb
## a single record from your old chums wings

**Apple 1851**

REGISTER TO VOTE/THE WORLD DEPENDS ON YOU

**'HI, HI, HI' / 'C MOON'**
**WINGS**
**UK release** December 1 1972; Apple R 5973; chart high No.5.
**US release** December 4 1972; Apple 1857; chart high No.10.

**'Hi, Hi, Hi' (Paul and Linda McCartney)**
Paul McCartney (vocals, bass), Linda McCartney (keyboard, backing vocals), Denny Laine (guitar), Henry McCullough (guitar), Denny Seiwell (drums).
**'C Moon' (Paul and Linda McCartney)**
Paul McCartney (vocals, piano, marimba), Linda McCartney (backing vocals, percussion), Denny Laine (bass), Henry McCullough (drums), Denny Seiwell (cornet, xylophone).
Both recorded at Morgan Studios, London, England. Both produced by Paul McCartney.

**'HI, HI, HI'**
On August 10 1972, immediately after Wings' performance at the Scandinavium Hall in Gothenburg, Sweden, Paul, Linda and Denny Seiwell were arrested for possession of marijuana. Customs officials had intercepted a parcel addressed to McCartney containing seven ounces of the dreaded weed. When questioned, all three denied any knowledge of either the parcel or the drugs. However, after around three hours of questioning, they confessed that drugs were being sent to them on a regular basis so they could avoid going through Customs with the drugs themselves.

John Morris, the band's tour manager, made a statement to the press on their behalf. "Paul, Linda, and Dennis did admit to the Swedish police that they used hash. At first they denied it, but the police gave them a rough time and started threatening all sorts of things. The police said they would bar the group from leaving the country unless they confessed." The musicians were released after paying around £1,000 in fines (about $2,500 at the time) and given the option of either leaving the country or continuing with the tour. They continued, as planned, with a concert in Lund.

McCartney later claimed that Wings use of drink and drugs on the '72 tour had been an experiment to discover whether or not they played better under the influence than when straight. "When we first came to Europe with the first line-up of Wings, this is where the stories about drinking came, [but] the truth is we were pretty out of it on stage. There was no discipline just in case that was a better way. We tried that, you know, maybe it's not so good to be disciplined, we'll try it the other way, and we tried, but we didn't play the music right. You'd have solos all out of tune, so it just wasn't worth being drunk for or high for."

Wings weren't the Grateful Dead or the Allman Brothers Band. As Henry McCullough discovered to his cost, McCartney was a disciplinarian who demanded rigid adherence to his arrangements each and every night. There was no room in Wings for musicians who liked to jam before a paying audience, that was something reserved for the studio. If Wings were taking drugs to affect their music it didn't work because as the hours of live bootleg recordings from that tour testify, Wings performed the same set and arrangements night after night, and they couldn't have done that if they were getting drunk or high before a gig. McCartney's attempt to explain his drug use might have been an elaborate ruse to disguise the fact that his consumption of drink and drugs had sky rocketed. He'd alluded to it in song and would later admit to it publicly.

Less than a month later, police inspected McCartney's farm in Scotland and found several marijuana plants. This time he was charged with knowingly cultivating the plants and ordered to appear in court the following March. Pleading guilty to possessing and having control of cannabis, once again McCartney claimed that the seeds had been sent to him through the post by a fan. McCartney was fined £100 ($250), but as this was his second bust in just over a month, he obviously expected a harsher sentence. Interviewed outside the court he joked: "I was planning on writing a few songs in jail."

McCartney wasn't documenting recent run-ins with the authorities but 'Hi, Hi, Hi' must surly have been tainted by his love of spliff. Written while holidaying in Spain for the band's upcoming tour it celebrated rock's Holy Trinity sex and drugs and rock'n'roll. Naturally the 'straights' at the BBC thought McCartney was endorsing communion with these teenage taboos, his recent run-ins with the authorities, for possession of marijuana, must have coloured their reaction. When asked about the song, McCartney claimed he wasn't being deliberately rebellious, just plain naïve. "[I thought] the 'Hi, Hi, Hi' thing could easily be taken as a natural high, could be taken as a booze high and everything. It doesn't have to be drugs, you know, so I'd kind of get away with it. Well, the first thing they saw was drugs, so I didn't get away with that." The record was banned but it did little harm to either his reputation or the record's sales. In fact in the short-term, McCartney's conviction for possession of cannabis made headline news around the world. An unnamed member of Wings allegedly said: "The police action against us was an excellent advertisement. Our name flies now all over the world." It may have seemed like a gas at the time, but his criminal record made getting into the USA that little bit more difficult.

If McCartney thought he could fool the censors into believing that 'Hi, Hi, Hi' was unrelated to any form of drug-induced high, the song's sexual innuendoes proved to be just as provocative. Due to no fault of his own, radio stations received incorrect copies of the lyrics. He said: "I just had some line, 'Lie on the bed get ready for my polygon.' The daft thing about all of that was our publishing company, Northern Songs, owned by Lew Grade, got the lyrics wrong and sent them round to the radio station, and it said, 'Get ready for my body gun,' which is far more suggestive than anything I put. 'Get ready for my polygon' – watch out baby. I mean it was suggestive, but abstract suggestive, which I thought I'd get away with. Bloody company goes round and makes it much more specific by putting 'body gun' – better words, almost." A classic McCartney rocker, 'Hi Hi Hi' has everything going for it: controversial lyrics, a solid performance, and a false ending that's as ripped as a speed freak's adrenaline rush.

'C Moon' finds Wings in reggae mode, and to keep things fresh the band swapped instruments. McCartney played piano and marimba, Linda tambourine and backing vocals, Henry McCullough drums, Denny Laine bass, and Denny Seiwell cornet. 'C Moon' seemed innocuous enough, but it too had a message. It was McCartney's coded way of saying everything was cool. Explaining the lyric to Sounds, he said: "Remember Sam The Sham and 'Woolly Bully'? Well, there's a line in that that says 'Let's not be L 7' – and at the time everyone was saying 'What's L 7 mean?' Well, L 7, it was explained at the time, means a square – put L and 7 together and you get a square. So I thought of the idea of putting a C and a crescent moon together to get the opposite of a square. So C Moon means cool."

### Hi, Hi, Hi' data

'Hi, Hi, Hi' / 'C Moon' was released in the UK by Apple Records as a double A-side single with customised red labels and a generic yellow Wings sleeve. Original British pressings carry the legend 'An Apple Record (P) 1972 The Gramophone Company Ltd. An EMI Recording' and publishing credits 'McCartney Music Limited Northern Songs Ltd'. Demonstration copies were issued with a large black 'A' at 2 o'clock and 'DEMO RECORD NOT FOR SALE' on three lines above the spindle hole.

When the single was reissued in the mid 1970s, the publishing credits were changed to 'McCartney Music Ltd by arrangement with ATV Music Ltd' and the reference to Apple Records replaced with '(P) 1972 MPL Communications Inc'. The reissue was manufactured with two label variations: red labels with black text, or black labels with silver text.

American pressings (issued with generic Apple sleeves) utilise the same label design as British pressings. The US reissue was manufactured with black and silver Capitol 'dome' labels. Apple did not prepare demonstration singles for the American release.

Mexican EP

Japanese single

Belgium single

EMI mid-70s reissue, subcontracted CBS Pressing

Capitol mid-70s reissue

Belgium picture sleeve

Mexican EP picture sleeve

Spanish picture sleeve

Danish picture sleeve

1973: My Love to Band On The Run

### 'MY LOVE' / 'THE MESS'
### PAUL McCARTNEY AND WINGS
**UK release** March 23 1973; Apple R 5985; chart high No.9.
**US release** April 9 1973; Apple 1861; chart high No.1.

### 'My Love' (McCartney)
Paul McCartney (vocals, electric piano), Linda McCartney (backing vocals), Denny Laine (bass), Henry McCullough (guitar), Denny Seiwell (drums). Recorded at AIR Studios or Abbey Road Studios, London, England.
### 'The Mess' (McCartney)
Paul McCartney (vocals, bass), Linda McCartney (keyboards, backing vocals), Denny Laine (guitar), Henry McCullough (guitar), Denny Seiwell (drums). Live recording at Congresgebouw, The Hague, Netherlands.
Both produced by Paul McCartney.


### 'MY LOVE'
While Lennon was writing about American politics and recording with a hard-nosed band of roughneck rockers, McCartney had been busy crafting a mix of twee pop songs, blistering rockers and honing Wings' studios skills to perfection. 'My Love' marked the beginning of Wings' mature period. The long hours spent rehearsing, touring and recording had knocked all the rough edges of the band which on record at least now sounded as polished as they had once sounded ragged. The restrained sensitivity of their playing, absent from much of the band's early material, indicated a growing self-assurance. For perhaps the first time Wings worked as a group, rather than a collective of individuals. 'My Love' featured some of the best ensemble playing that Wings Mk.2 ever recorded and was proof, if needed, that they were capable of creating work on a par with that of The Beatles. Unfortunately, this was to be the exception rather than the rule; inconsistencies dogged the forthcoming *Red Rose Speedway* album, as they would much of McCartney's solo career.

Taken from *Red Rose Speedway*, 'My Love' was recorded live in the studio, with a full orchestra, and features a sublime guitar solo by Henry McCullough. But as confident and fluid as it sounds, McCullough struggled with his performance. Perhaps it was recording with a full orchestra, or the pressure of trying to meet McCartney's exacting standards, but, as McCullough recalled: "Whenever the orchestra struck up, I took fright." For once, McCartney didn't blow his top but encouraged the guitarist to try something different. Speaking to Richard Skinner, McCartney said: "We'd worked it out and rehearsed it, and we had a full orchestra, it was … played and sung live. We had the whole orchestra waiting … for the downbeat and Henry McCullough, the Irish guitar player, comes over to me and says, 'Just a minute, do you mind if I change the solo?' And actually it's one of the best solos he ever played."

Wings were cooking. All the false starts, hard work and low budget touring was beginning to pay off. Speaking to *Melody Maker* only weeks after the single had been released, McCullouch said: "The band has really progressed as a team. Everybody wants to make it as a band, whereas before it was just Paul. Wings has all the makings of a great group, but our battle is to keep it as a band and not let it fall apart as it could so easily do. It's worth going at it. I'm there 100 per cent, I know we've got a lot to offer."

'The Mess' was an example of McCartney's other strength: heads-down-no-nonsense rock'n'roll. Recorded live in The Hague, it was one of the stronger songs Wings showcased during their 1972 European tour. Several other songs performed during the tour, such as '1882' and 'Best Friend', were also recorded and prepared for release, but only 'The Mess' made it onto record. McCartney attempted a studio version, but was unhappy with the results and decided to overdub onto the live version and edit that for release.

### 'My Love' data
Apple issued Wings' forth single in Britain with customised 'Red Rose Speedway' labels with a red paper sleeve. It came with two label variations: the first has the artist credit 'Paul McCartney & Wings'; the second 'McCartney's Wings'. Demonstration copies of the single were issued with a large silver 'A' at 4 o'clock and 'DEMO RECORD NOT FOR SALE' on three lines above the spindle hole.

The single was reissued in the mid 1970s with customised 'Red Rose Speedway' labels but without reference to Apple Records and publisher credits altered to 'McCartney Music by arr. with ATV Music Ltd'.

American pressings of the single were issued with the same label design as the British single, with the addition of 'Recorded In England', in generic Apple sleeves. White-label promotional singles with the song title, composer credit, artist, and copyright information printed in black text were issued to radio stations.

Billboard, Cash Box
and
RECORD WORLD
agree...
MY LOVE
is the #1 single
RED ROSE SPEEDWAY
is the #1 album...

and Wings' next #1 single
will be McCartney's
LIVE AND LET DIE

Apple Single 1863

The US single was reissued in the mid 1970s with black and silver Capitol 'dome' labels. When McCartney signed with Columbia in the USA, the company reissued several new couplings of classic McCartney/Wings songs on their Hall Of Fame imprint. 'My Love' was coupled with 'Maybe I'm Amazed' (13-33407) and issued with red Columbia labels and, later, with grey labels.

*RED ROSE SPEEDWAY*
PAUL McCARTNEY AND WINGS
**Side 1** 'Big Barn Bed', 'My Love', 'Get On The Right Thing', 'One More Kiss', 'Little Lamb Dragonfly'.
**Side 2** 'Single Pigeon', 'When The Night', 'Loop (1st Indian On The Moon)', 'Medley: Hold Me Tight/Lazy Dynamite/Hands Of Love/Power Cut'.
**UK release** May 3 1973; LP Apple PCTC 251; 8-track cartridge Apple 8X-PCTC 251 released May 3 1973; chart high No.4.
**US release** April 30 1973; LP Apple SMAL-3409; 8-track cartridge Apple 8XW 3409; chart high No.1.

**'Big Barn Bed' (McCartney)**
Paul McCartney (vocals, piano, bass), Linda McCartney (backing vocals), Denny Laine (guitar, backing vocals), Henry McCullough (guitar, backing vocals), Denny Seiwell (drums).
**'Get On The Right Thing' (McCartney)**
Paul McCartney (vocals, bass, piano), Linda McCartney (backing vocals), Dave Spinoza (guitar), Denny Seiwell (drums).
**'One More Kiss' (McCartney)**
Paul McCartney (vocals, guitar), Linda McCartney (electric harpsichord), Denny Laine (bass), Henry McCullough (guitar), Denny Seiwell (drums).
**'Little Lamb Dragonfly' (McCartney)**
Paul McCartney (vocals, bass), Linda McCartney (dingers, backing vocals), Denny Laine (backing vocals), Hugh McCracken (guitar), Denny Seiwell (drums).
**'Single Pigeon' (McCartney)**
Paul McCartney (vocals, piano), Linda McCartney (backing vocals), Denny Laine (drums), Henry McCullough (guitar), Denny Seiwell (bass).
**'When The Night' (McCartney)**
Paul McCartney (vocals, piano), Linda McCartney (piano, backing vocals), Denny Laine (guitar, backing vocals), Henry McCullough (guitar, backing vocals), Denny Seiwell (drums, backing vocals).
**'Loop (1st Indian On The Moon)' (McCartney)**
Paul McCartney (bass, guitar, Moog, chant), Linda McCartney (organ, chant), Denny Laine (guitar, chant), Henry McCullough (guitar, chant), Denny Seiwell (drums, chant).
**'Medley: Hold Me Tight/Lazy Dynamite/Hands Of Love/Power Cut' (McCartney)**
Hold Me Tight: Paul McCartney (bass, piano, vocals), Linda McCartney (backing vocals), Denny Laine (guitar, backing vocals), Henry McCullough (guitar, backing vocals), Denny Seiwell (drums, backing vocals); Lazy Dynamite: Paul McCartney (bass, piano, Mellotron, vocals), Denny Laine (harmonica), Henry McCullough (guitar); Hands Of Love: Paul McCartney (guitar, vocals), Linda McCartney (backing vocals), Denny Laine (guitar), Henry McCullough (percussion), Denny Seiwell (drums, percussion); Power Cut: Paul McCartney (piano, celeste, Mellotron, vocals), Linda McCartney (electric piano), Denny Laine (guitar, backing vocals), Henry McCullough (guitar, backing vocals), Denny Seiwell (drums).
All recorded at Olympic Sound Studios, Barnes, England, except: 'Get On The Right Thing' and 'Little Lamb Dragonfly' recorded at A&R Studios and Columbia Studios, New York City, NY, USA; and 'One more Kiss' recording location unknown. All produced by Paul McCartney.

RED ROSE SPEEDWAY

Released to coincide with Wings' 1973 British tour, *Red Rose Speedway* was better conceived, performed, and produced than their debut album. However, while Linda claimed that they had some 30 songs to choose from – the album was originally planned as a double – much of what McCartney decided to include was lightweight and pedestrian. Interviewed after its release, Linda said: "*Red Rose Speedway* was such a non-confident record ... . We needed a heavier sound. ... It was a terribly unsure period."

Still searching for his sonic signature, McCartney was desperate to produce a defining statement to free himself from the long shadow cast by The Beatles. Unfortunately, *Red Rose Speedway* failed to provide Wings with the grounding they required to compete with much of the contemporary competition, let alone the Fab Four. One reason the album sounds so over produced is because McCartney felt he had to give the band parts to play even if they were superfluous. However, his attempts to keep everybody happy worked against him. "Paul got very nervous having to give everyone in the band a part to play," explained Linda. "Sometimes he wouldn't want guitar on a track but Henry [McCullough] didn't like sitting around the studio. Because of that Paul started putting things on tracks on the *Red Rose Speedway* album just to keep everyone happy, things he wouldn't normally put on the track."

Recorded between March and October 1972, the original double album was to have included contributions from Denny Laine and Linda. Laine's 'I Would Only Smile' was later released on his solo album *Japanese Tears*. Linda's 'Seaside Woman' was earmarked for the album (work on the song began at AIR Studios, London, in November 1972), but the song remained unreleased until issued as a single in America in 1977 and didn't appear in Britain until 1980. Also recorded but dropped from the album were 'Night Out' – which McCartney continued to work on throughout the 1970s – 'Jazz Street', 'Thank You Darling', and a cover of Thomas Wayne's 'Tragedy'. 'Night Out' and 'Tragedy' were later scheduled for the *Cold Cuts* album, which McCartney planned to release on several occasions until the bootleggers beat him to it, whereupon he lost interest in the project.

Rather than release an expensive and possibly less commercial double LP, *Red Rose Speedway* was condensed to a single album. According to McCullough, McCartney was persuaded to do this by business advisors. Speaking in 1994, McCullough recalled his disappointment at the album's final running order. "I'd been really delighted, because from what you heard on the album, there was another side to it that brought out the best in McCartney. And I thought, 'Great, at last he's doing something that my friends are going to like!' He was starting to rock out a little bit. But it only came out as a single and the rest was never released."

### Red Rose Speedway songs

The opening track, 'Big Barn Bed', was recorded at Olympic Studios but harks back to *Ram*. The opening stanza first appeared as part of the reprise of 'Ram On' and was recycled for this rambling contrapuntal composition. Recycling lyrics from old songs, whether his own or others, was a trick McCartney used when sketching in sections of a song that were proving difficult to finish. Talking to Miles about songwriting, he said: "Often you just block songs out and words just come into your mind, and when they do, it's hard to get rid of them. You often quote other songs too, and you know you've got to get rid of them, but sometimes it's very difficult to find a more suitable phrase than the one that had insinuated itself into your consciousness." Unable to better the lyric borrowed from 'Ram On', McCartney stuck with his original idea. The result was that, lyrically, 'Big Barn Bed' remained little more than an undeveloped fragment that went nowhere.

Although McCartney had more than enough material for a double album for some reason he selected two outtakes from *Ram* to pad out the album. 'Get On The Right Thing' is hippie heaven – oneness with nature, sunshine, the wife and kids, and love sweet love – and McCartney the proselytiser wants to spread the word. Unfortunately, we've heard it all before and better.

'One More Kiss' is a simple country song that fails to bring anything new to the album. Ironically, superior country-flavoured material recorded during these sessions appeared as future B-sides, which is where McCartney should have buried 'One More Kiss'.

Before it was released on *Red Rose Speedway*, 'Little Lamb Dragonfly' had been pencilled in for an early version of McCartney's proposed Rupert Bear film. Recorded while making *Ram*, it's marginally better than much of what was selected for the album, but it still fails to satisfy. McCartney's decision to revisit the song was perhaps a recognition that something had to be done to save a flagging project, but it was too little too late. 'Little Lamb Dragonfly' is too cute for its own good and merely confirms the earlier observation that McCartney was trying to be all things to all men, women, and little lambs.

'Single Pigeon' found the band swapping instruments as they had with 'C Moon'. McCartney plays piano and sings lead, Laine plays drums, and Seiwell bass guitar; McCullough is absent as no guitar part was required. This song was far from inspired and eventually fell into the category of 'post-Beatles stuff' that McCartney all but disowned. "The Beatles were possibly the hardest act of all to follow," he recalled. "So Linda and I fell in with everyone else's opinion of it – which was that it was not as good as The Beatles, therefore it was no good at all. I hated a lot of the songs from that period."

When writing for others, particularly early in his career, McCartney turned out some particularly asinine lyrics – 'One And One Is Two,' mainly written by McCartney and given to The Strangers with Mike Shannon, is one such example. Thankfully, few of the songs he chose to record himself have been quite as senseless. Unfortunately, the same cannot be said 'When The Night', which is fatuous in the extreme.

Having struggled through side one and then half of side two, the listener encounters a laboured and undistinguished instrumental, 'Loop (1st Indian On The Moon)'. The band chant block harmonies, guitars chime, organs hum, and the whole thing plods aimlessly along like a bad Pink Floyd outtake. There's some attempt at dynamic interplay midway through before it lurches back into full swing (or should that be full plod?), but even this fails to awake this tired instrumental from its spiritless slumber. Nobody gets a decent solo, which in the light of McCullough's exceptional solo on 'My Love' seems strange indeed.

The album closes *Abbey Road*-style with a long medley. However, unlike the *Abbey Road* medley, which gives the impression of totality, the *Red Rose Speedway* medley simply emphasises the disparate nature of McCartney's song fragments. In fact, it's probably better to consider the four 'songs' – 'Hold Me Tight', 'Lazy Dynamite', 'Hands Of Love', and 'Power Cut' – as individual compositions rather than a suite of songs. Why McCartney bothered to construct a medley from these scraps when he had superior finished songs to choose from is a mystery. Perhaps it was an attempt to recapture the magic of *Abbey Road* – McCartney's favourite moment from that album was the long medley – but on this occasion it failed.

'Hold Me Tight' consists of little more than the title repeated over a pleasant but uninspired tune. 'Lazy Dynamite' isn't much better. Only McCartney, McCullough, and Seiwell, who adds harmonica, play on the track; although drums are present, the drummer is uncredited. A guitar fanfare links 'Lazy Dynamite' with 'Hands Of Love' but this conceit was accomplished with more panache on *Abbey Road*, where a similar approach was used to join 'Mean Mr Mustard' with 'Polythene Pam'. Deployed here it sounds clumsy and amateurish. The medley ends with 'Power Cut', cross-faded from 'Hands Of Love'. As Wings toured Britain in 1973, the country was in the grip of large-scale industrial unrest. A three-day working week had been introduced, with the result that the country often suffered power cuts. Interviewed for *Billboard* magazine in 2001, McCartney suggested that 'Power Cut' was written in response to these disruptions. Finally, in an attempt to create some form of musical unity, the main motifs from the previous three songs are repeated to bring the medley, and the album, to an end.

### Red Rose Speedway data
*Red Rose Speedway* was issued in Britain with customised labels featuring a 'Red Rose Speedway' logo, a gatefold jacket, and an elaborate six-page colour booklet featuring photos of Wings in concert and on a trip to Marrakech. McCartney also employed the talents of two of Britain's leading artists to create artwork for the booklet, Alan Jones and Eduardo Paolozzi (contemporaries of Peter Blake and Richard Hamilton, who created the *Sgt Pepper* and *White Album* covers). American pressings of the LP were also issued with 'Red Rose Speedway' labels but with the addition of the band's new logo. Capitol produced a 3 3/4-inch by 1 7/8-inch rectangular blue label with 'PAUL McCARTNEY AND WINGS' and the track listing, which was stuck to the front cover.

Original sleeves featured a Braille message that read, 'We love ya baby', a tribute to the McCartneys' favourite singer, Stevie Wonder. And for the first time, the address of Wings Fun Club, which ran until 1998, was printed on the sleeve. The album was issued on 8-track in Britain (8X-PCTC 251) and the USA (8XW 3409). When McCartney signed with Columbia in the 1980s it reissued the 8-track (JCA 36481).

EMI reissued the LP on its FAME imprint (FA 3193) on September 5 1987 without the Braille message or booklet. Columbia also reissued the LP, as FC-36481 and PC-36481. *Red Rose Speedway* was issued on CD by EMI on its FAME imprint on October 5 1987 (CD-FA 3193) and by Capitol in November 1988 (CDM 7 52026 2). EMI issued a remastered CD (CDPMCOL4) on July 7 1993 and DCC Compact Classics issued a gold CD (GZS-1091) in 1996.

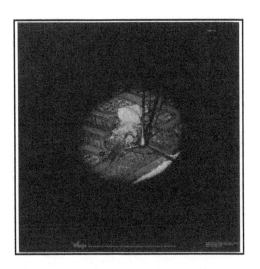

UK issue

US issue

New Zealand issue

## 'LIVE AND LET DIE' / 'I LIE AROUND'
## WINGS
**UK release** June 1 1973; Apple R 5987; chart high No.9.
**US release** June 18 1973; Apple 1863; chart high No.1.

### 'Live And Let Die' (McCartney)
Paul McCartney (piano, vocals), Linda McCartney (keyboards, backing vocals), Denny Laine (bass, backing vocals), Henry McCullough (guitar), Denny Seiwell (drums). Recorded at AIR Studios, London, England. Produced by George Martin.

### 'I Lie Around' (McCartney)
Paul McCartney (bass, backing vocals), Linda McCartney (backing vocals), Denny Laine (guitar, vocals), Henry McCullough (guitar), Denny Seiwell (drums). Recording location unknown, probably Olympic Studios, London.
Produced by Paul McCartney.

### 'LIVE AND LET DIE'
Recorded in October 1972 while completing *Red Rose Speedway*, 'Live And Let Die' was everything the album wasn't. Powerful, atmospheric and dymanic 'Live And Let Die' was commissioned by the film's producer, Albert 'Chubby' Broccoli. Although McCartney was asked to write the song, Broccoli wanted another artist to record it. However, McCartney and George Martin had other plans. "George took it out to the Caribbean," said McCartney, "where they were shooting the movie, and the film producers found a record player. After the record had finished they said to George, 'That's great, a wonderful demo. Now when are you going to make the real track, and who shall we get to sing it?' And George said, 'What? This is the real track!'" The misunderstanding rectified, Wings' recording featured in the film.

Attention-grabbing theme songs are an essential part of the Bond formula. The original James Bond theme, arranged by John Barry, provided a dynamic, electrifying introduction to Ian Fleming's action-packed spy thrillers. McCartney's theme not only captures the excitement of a Bond movie but also fits perfectly into the Bond template.

Recalling how he came to write the song, McCartney said: "I read the *Live And Let Die* book on a Saturday, got the feel of it, and on the Sunday sat down at the piano and wrote the music. Linda and I dug around with the words for a bit, then I asked George Martin if he'd produce it, and we recorded it with Wings, all mixed all proper, as you hear it in the film." McCartney knew instinctively that Martin was the ideal producer to help realise the song. Martin's experience as an arranger and producer was unequalled: if anyone could write a score to compliment McCartney's dynamic song, it was him.

McCartney and Martin's arrangement uses the full dynamic range of orchestra and band to create a dramatic soundscape that echoes Bond's on-screen image. Beginning with a simple piano and vocal introduction, that lulls the listener into a false sense of security, the music explodes with a monster riff that conveys all the excitement and action one expects of a Bond movie. Linda even managed to put a 'reggae' middle eight into the song, which lightens the mood a little before the thunderous riff re-emerges with stunning effect. 'Live And Let Die' quickly became a live favourite and remained in McCartney's live set from the mid 1970s well into the 21st century and appears on all his live albums.

'I Lie Around' was written by McCartney but sung by Denny Laine and finds its author extolling the virtues of a bucolic lifestyle. The countryside is again conceived of as a place of tranquillity and escape, where troubles and anxieties are forgotten. It was recorded during sessions for *Red Rose Speedway* and benefits from a sympathetic arrangement that compliments McCartney's musings on nature as a mental restorative.

### 'Live And Let Die' data

'Live And Let Die' was issued with generic Apple labels rather than the customary bespoke design McCartney had employed for Wings' releases. Perhaps, now that Klein had departed, McCartney felt more comfortable with Apple and more willing to associate himself with the label.

Three label variations were issued in America. The first has a light green Apple label with 'STEREO' at 9 o'clock and 'Recorded in England' below; title, '(from the United Artists film "Live and Let Die")', composer, and band name are centre bottom. The second label variant has a light green Apple label; '(from the United Artists film "Live and Let Die") at 10 o'clock; 'STEREO' at 9 o'clock with the Intro. and Total running times printed below; title, composer, band name, and 'Recorded in England' centre bottom.

The third variant has the same label layout at the second but substitutes "Unart Music Corporation" for "United Artist Music Corp., Inc.".

'Live And Let Die' was reissued by EMI and Capitol in the mid 1970s with black and silver Capitol 'dome' labels.

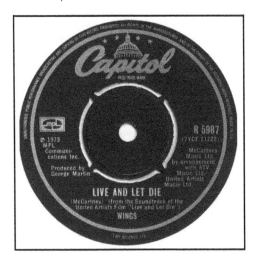

'HELEN WHEELS' / 'COUNTRY DREAMER'
PAUL McCARTNEY AND WINGS
**UK release** October 26 1973; Apple R 5993; chart high No.12.
**US release** November 12 1973; Apple 1869; chart high No.10.

### 'Helen Wheels' (McCartney)

Paul McCartney (bass, drums, vocals), Linda McCartney (keyboards, backing vocals), Denny Laine (guitar, backing vocals). Recorded at EMI and ARC Studios, Lagos, Nigeria; mixed at Kingsway Studios, London, England.

### 'Country Dreamer' (McCartney)

Paul McCartney (bass, vocals), Linda McCartney (backing vocals), Denny Laine (guitar, backing vocals), Henry McCullough (guitar), Denny Seiwell (drums). Recording location unknown, probably Olympic Studios, London.
Both produced by Paul McCartney.

### 'HELEN WHEELS'

'Helen Wheels' was McCartney's ode to the road. A song about travelling from his home in Scotland to London, it was inspired by an unlikely source – his car. "'Helen Wheels is … a name we gave to our Land Rover, which is a trusty vehicle that gets us around Scotland," he explained. "It takes us up to the Shetland Islands and down to London. The song starts off in Glasgow, then it goes past Carlisle, goes to Kendal, Liverpool, Birmingham, and London. It's the route coming down from our Scottish farm to London. So it's really the story of a trip down." However, the song is more than an account of a road journey. It's a metaphor for McCartney's desire to escape the pressures of fame and running a band, and it mirrors similar themes (movement, escape, freedom) that he'd explore in greater depth on *Band On The Run*.

'Country Dreamer' is another song about the pleasures that McCartney found in the countryside, recorded late in 1972 during sessions for *Red Rose Speedway*. In light of that album's heavy-handed production, the economic arrangement and sensitive production of 'Country Dreamer' was refreshingly honest.

### 'Helen Wheels' data

Apple issued 'Helen Wheels' with generic labels in a black paper sleeve. There were three label variations for US releases. The first has a light green Apple label with 'STEREO' at 9 o'clock and Intro and Total running times directly above; title, composer, band name, and producer credits are centre bottom. The second has a dark green Apple label with the same layout. The third US label variant has a dark green Apple label with 'STEREO' at 9 o'clock; Intro. and Total running times printed on right side of label directly above catalogue number; title, composer, band name, and producer credits centre bottom. Demonstration copies (PRO-6786) of the A-side (mono/stereo) were issued in America with light green Apple labels. The A-side label has 'MONO' at 9 o'clock with 'NOT FOR SALE' printed below. 'Country Dreamer' was also issued as a mono/stereo demonstration single (PRO-6787) with light green Apple labels with a black star at 7 o'clock. A third demonstration single, with stereo versions of both A and B-sides, was also issued (P-1869).

In Britain, Apple issued demonstration copies with a large 'A' at 2 o'clock and 'DEMO RECORD NOT FOR SALE' on three lines above the spindle hole. 'Helen Wheels' / 'Country Dreamer' was reissued by EMI and Capitol in the mid 1970s with black and silver Capitol 'dome' labels.

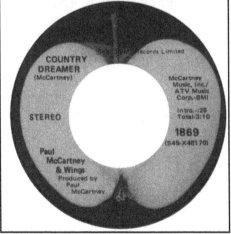

## BAND ON THE RUN
### PAUL McCARTNEY AND WINGS
**Side 1** 'Band On The Run', 'Jet', 'Bluebird', 'Mrs Vandebilt', 'Let Me Roll It'.
**Side 2** 'Mamunia', 'No Words', 'Helen Wheels' (US edition only), 'Picasso's Last Words (Drink To Me)', 'Nineteen Hundred And Eighty Five'.
**UK release** November 30 1973; LP Apple PAS 10007; 8-track cartridge Apple 8X-PAS 10007 released January 1974; chart high No.1.
**US release** December 3 1973; LP Apple SO-3415; 8-track cartridge Apple 8XZ3415; quadraphonic 8-track cartridge Apple Q8W-3415; chart high No.1.

**'Band On The Run' (McCartney)**
Paul McCartney (bass, guitar, drums, vocals), Linda McCartney (keyboards, backing vocals), Denny Laine (guitar, backing vocals).
**'Jet' (McCartney)**
Paul McCartney (bass, guitar, drums, vocals), Linda McCartney (keyboards, backing vocals), Denny Laine (guitar, backing vocals).
**'Bluebird' (McCartney)**
Paul McCartney (guitar, vocals), Linda McCartney (backing vocals), Denny Laine (guitar, backing vocals), Remi Kebaka (percussion), Howie Casey (saxophone).
**'Mrs Vandebilt' (McCartney)**
Paul McCartney (bass, guitar, drums, vocals), Linda McCartney (backing vocals), Denny Laine (guitar, backing vocals).
**'Let Me Roll It' (McCartney)**
Paul McCartney (bass, guitar, drums, vocals), Linda McCartney (keyboards, backing vocals), Denny Laine (guitar, backing vocals).
**'Mamunia' (McCartney)**
Paul McCartney (bass, guitar, vocals), Linda McCartney (backing vocals), Denny Laine (guitar, backing vocals).
**'No Words' (McCartney, Laine)**
Paul McCartney (bass, guitar, drums, vocals), Linda McCartney (vocals), Denny Laine (guitar, vocals), Ian Horne & Trevor Jones (backing vocals).
**'Picasso's Last Words (Drink To Me)' (McCartney)**
Paul McCartney (bass, keyboards, guitar, vocals), Linda McCartney (backing vocals), Denny Laine (guitar, vocals), Ginger Baker (percussion).
**'Nineteen Hundred And Eighty Five' (McCartney)**
Paul McCartney (bass, piano, guitar, vocals), Linda McCartney (keyboards, backing vocals), Denny Laine (guitar, vocals).
All recorded EMI Studios, Lagos, Nigeria and AIR Studios, London, England and mixed at Kingsway Studios, London, except 'Jet' recorded at Abbey Road and AIR Studios, London, England. All produced by Paul McCartney.

BAND ON THE RUN

With the issue of *Band On The Run* just two weeks after Lennon's *Mind Games*, Liverpool's two most famous sons were competing for album sales and chart superiority. As Lennon had a hit single he should have had the advantage, but McCartney would eventually emerge as the winner. Wings' first LP to reach Number 1 on both sides of the Atlantic, *Band On The Run* became the most successful album by any of the ex-Beatles. It spawned two Top 10 singles – three in America, where 'Helen Wheels' was included – and, in stark contrast to the withering disdain normally reserved for McCartney, it received glowing reviews. *Rolling Stone* magazine made it album of the year and couldn't praise it enough. The magazine suggested that McCartney's new assuredness resulted from his "uniting the myth of the rock star and the outlaw, the original legendary figure On The Run."

If previous albums had stretched McCartney and Wings, recording *Band On The Run* was going to push them to the very limits of endurance. Just as things were looking up for Wings, disaster struck. On the eve of Wings' departure for recording in Lagos, Nigeria, guitarist Henry McCullough and drummer Denny Seiwell left the band. Neither saw a secure future with Wings. Speaking to *Melody Maker* in April 1973, McCullough said: "I don't suppose we'll be together forever; I'm sure Paul's got more of a tie to The Beatles than to Wings." As The Beatles' business troubles were being resolved, McCullough obviously thought that a reunion was a real possibility. He was also unhappy with his role in the band. When he made his feelings known to *Disc*, the music paper ran the headline: "McCullough To Quit Wings?" McCullough wanted more freedom and to contribute more ideas to the band. For him, being in Wings felt like being bound in a straightjacket. Recalling his time with the band, McCullough said: "It was like being in a show band – you played the exact same thing as the record, and you played it every night from there on in."

Despite his love of improvisation, McCartney demanded strict adherence to formal arrangements when performing in front of an audience. McCullough, however, felt stifled; for him, playing live was the musical equivalent of flying by the seat of your pants. Linda's presence didn't help, either. As she would have been the first to acknowledge, her musical inexperience undoubtedly caused friction within the group, as did the fact that she was the boss's wife. McCullough was quoted as saying: "Trying to get things together with a learner in the group didn't work as far as I was concerned."

McCullough's departure was put down to musical differences, and McCartney was pragmatic about his departure. "I think Henry McCullough came to a head one day when I asked him to play something he really didn't fancy playing. We all got a bit choked about it, and he rang up later and said he was leaving. I said, 'Well OK.' That's how that happened. You know, with the kind of music we play, a guitarist has got to be adaptable. It was just one of those things."

In April 1973, McCartney intimated that a Beatles reunion was a possibility. "The only thing that has prevented us from getting together again has been Klein's contractual hold over The Beatles' name; when he is out of the way, there is no real reason why we shouldn't get together again." The remark did little to ease relations within Wings. McCartney seems to have overlooked the fact that for Laine, McCullough and Seiwell, Wings paid the rent. If McCartney decided to get The Beatles back together they'd be out of a job. Speaking to *Record Mirror*, Seiwell said: "Now that the obstruction in the form of Allen Klein has gone, I should think that there's a strong possibility that they will all get together again."

Klein's departure must have weighed on Seiwell's mind for only hours before he was due to leave with the McCartneys for Lagos he informed them was leaving the band. McCartney: "So our drummer didn't want to go to Africa. I don't know quite why. We're all going to Africa to record and if the drummer won't come, what do you do?" McCullough and Seiwell's departure might have marked the end of Wings Mk.2, but it signalled another rebirth from which a newly invigorated band would rise phoenix-like from the ashes. As Linda recalled: "That period was almost a relief for Paul. He finally had people with him who cared, those who showed up at the airport. We didn't even know if Denny (Laine) was coming."

The set of recordings that resulted were not only a triumph of will over adversity, but, perhaps because of the pressure under which they were made, some of Paul, Linda and Denny's most creative and commercial recordings. Speaking to *Melody Maker*, McCartney said: "'Oh Jesus,' I thought, 'this is it, either we go under here or we make a good album.' And I think we made a good album."

*Band On The Run* was the first of several McCartney/Wings albums recorded in 'exotic' locations. *Band On The Run* was made at EMI Studios in Lagos and AIR Studios, London. McCartney's desire to record in a foreign location was, nevertheless, tempered by the need for technical excellence, which he believed an EMI studio would offer. As he explained: "I was at EMI and I'd been used to recording at their places, so I thought that any studio that EMI built I'd be able to relate to, the condition would be OK." However, when Wings reached Lagos their expectations were shattered. The studio, which backed onto a noisy pressing plant, was still under construction. Far from meeting EMI's high standards, it was Jerry built. There was no backup equipment, no acoustic screens (used to stop one instrument's sound bleeding into another microphone), and in fact there appeared to be no microphones at all, until some were discovered in a cardboard box hidden inside a cupboard. And to top it off, the mixing desk was faulty. But McCartney had hedged his bets: he took ex-Beatles engineer Geoff Emerick with him to engineer the sessions. It was Emerick's skills as an engineer that helped save the album from disaster.

McCartney's initial reason for recording in Lagos was to bring the region's music to a wider audience. His good intentions were, however, viewed with suspicion by local musicians, who thought he only wanted to steal their rhythms and create a diluted, Westernised version of *their* music for commercial gain. Fela Kuti, in particular, suspected that McCartney was there to exploit indigenous music at the expense of local musicians. McCartney recalled: "I think old Fela, when he found us in Lagos, thought, 'Hello, why have they come to Lagos?' And the only reason he could think of was that we must be stealing black music, black African music, the Lagos sound: we'd come down there to pick it up. So I said, 'Do us a favour, we do OK as it is, we're not pinching your music.'"

Although McCartney thought about employing African musicians, particularly a drummer to replace Denny Seiwell, he decided against it, realising that "it would have taken hours to tell [a new musician] exactly what I wanted. I knew basically that I could do most of it".

If antagonism from local musicians wasn't enough, Paul and Linda were mugged one evening while on their way to Denny's rented house. The couple were followed by a kerb-crawling car, out of which emerged a gang of muggers. Speaking to the *Daily Express* in 1977, McCartney said: "The doors flew open and they all came out (there were six of them) and one had a knife. Their eyes were wild and Linda was screaming: 'He's a musician! Don't kill him!' You know, all the unreasonable stuff you shout in situations like that." The McCartneys were lucky to lose only some money and cassettes containing demos of songs intended for the album; they could have lost their lives.

The stress was beginning to affect McCartney health and one evening he suffered another unsettling incident. Stepping into the Lagos night for a breath of air, he found that the atmosphere outside was more oppressive than in the studio. A sharp pain spread across the right side of his chest and he collapsed. When he awoke, he discovered that a local doctor was treating his condition somewhat casually. Ordered to bed for a few days, he thought he was dying. Thankfully, McCartney wasn't suffering from any serious illness and, after spending the weekend resting, returned to the recording studio to continue work on the album.

When they got back to England, Wings continued recording throughout September and October at AIR Studios in London, where the original 8-track tapes were transferred to 16-track to facilitate the overdubbing of Tony Visconti's orchestral arrangements. Compared with the band's previous album, sessions for which stretched over several months, *Band On The Run* was completed surprisingly quickly. In a few weeks, McCartney had created confident, well-crafted songs and bold musical settings that matched his mood. Whereas *Wild Life* and *Red Rose Speedway* represent opposing manifestations of taste and style, *Band On The Run* fused his sensibility and talents into a near perfect whole that had one critic enthusing that it was "the best thing any of The Beatles have done since *Abbey Road*". *Band On The Run* secured McCartney's post-Beatles reputation, as *Imagine* had for Lennon. But Lennon had peaked early, and by 1973 he had hit a creative doldrums. As Lennon began to drift, McCartney focused and honed his career, to the extent that Wings would soon rival The Beatles in popularity.

### Band On The Run songs

The album starts with the title track, a five-minute mini-opera with all the magnificence but none of the pretensions that too often trouble this particular rock genre, as McCartney explores his desire for freedom. McCartney was inspired to write the song by a chance remark that George Harrison made at an Apple business meeting. "He was saying that we were all prisoners in some way, some kind of remark like that. 'If we ever get out of here,' the prison bit ... and I thought that would be a nice way to start an album." George's comment neatly summarised The Beatles' business predicament, but had universal meaning. All of us are trying to escape reality for some imagined better place. McCartney simply took Harrison's offhand quip and turned it into a powerful metaphor for transcendence and deliverance.

He weaves together a number of melodic themes, examining contrasting responses to our attachment to freedom. First, we are confronted by despair at being incarcerated in a prison of our own making. Then a dramatic tempo change signals a declaration of intent, and finally a triumphant orchestral ostinato and dramatic change in timbre signifies hope. However, unlike Lennon's meditations on the subject, McCartney's vision is racked by doubt. Haunted by a succession of authority figures – jailer man (the law), sailor Sam (the armed forces), and an undertaker (death) – McCartney neither sees nor offers a solution to the problem. For him the pot of gold will forever be at the end of a rainbow, always over the next horizon, always out of reach.

When McCartney released *Band On The Run*, he insisted that it would stand on its own merits and that no singles would be issued from it. Although it had been selling well, it wasn't until 'Jet' was selected for release as a single that the album established itself at the top of the album charts. Released in November 1973, the album didn't reach Number 1 in Britain until the first week of July 1974, some eight months after its release. Persuaded by radio plugger Al Coury, McCartney conceded and issued 'Jet' as a single. He had written the song in Scotland after watching one of his dogs at play. "We've got a Labrador puppy who is a runt, the runt of the litter," he said. "She was a bit of a wild dog, a wild girl who wouldn't stay in. She came back one day pregnant. She proceeded to walk into the garage and have this litter. So, Jet was one of the puppies. We gave them all names, there was one puppy called Golden Molasses. I rather like that." But this is where inspiration ends and invention begins. Make of the lyrics what you will: they were probably written to fit the melody without much consideration for meaning. Even the suffragette motif was, likely as not, arrived at fortuitously. "I make up so much stuff," McCartney revealed. "It means something to me when I do it, and it means something to the record buyer, but if I'm asked to analyse it I can't really explain what it is. 'Suffragette' was crazy enough to work. It sounded silly, so I liked it."

Just as he was unhappy about lifting any singles from the album, McCartney was also unhappy about having his songs edited. If any songs were to be released as singles, he wanted them issued as they stood. However, at just over four minutes, 'Jet' was too long for most radio stations, who refused to play anything much over two minutes in length. After much persuasion, a McCartney-sanctioned edit was issued to American radio stations (Apple PRO-6827) and the single duly hit Number 1. Pop songs don't get much better than this: 'Jet' is as exuberant and vital as the Labrador puppy that inspired it.

'Bluebird' continues the album's theme of personal and spiritual emancipation. McCartney wrote it while on holiday in Jamaica, fashioning a metaphor for the transcendent power of love and the liberation of the human spirit from mental and physical bondage. His lyric reflects his transformation from traumatised to revitalised individual and maps a dramatic change in his general disposition. Enhanced by Howie Casey's warm saxophone, 'Bluebird' is an island of serenity in an equally calm sea. ('Bluebird' was issued as a single in Germany [1 C 006-05 529].)

'Mrs Vandebilt' finds McCartney asking the question, "What's the use of worrying?" and answering himself, "No use." Advancing a positive and optimistic attitude, the song finds him casting off his mantle of despair and revealing a more confident, carefree persona. Recording during a power cut, Paul, Denny and Linda found themselves relying on a noisy EMI generator, which they hoped wouldn't leak onto the backing track.

McCartney wrote 'Let Me Roll It' at home on his farm in Scotland. It's a stark Lennonesque track with a stripped-down arrangement, heavy rhythm section, and jagged guitar riff, which led many to believe that McCartney was somehow criticising his former partner. Lennonesque it may be, but McCartney was adamant that any similarities were purely coincidental. "*Let Me Roll It* was not really a Lennon pastiche, although my use of tape echo did sound more like John than me," he explained. "But tape echo was not John's exclusive territory. And you have to remember that, despite the myth, there was a lot of commonality between us in the way we thought and the way we worked."

Comparisons with Lennon were inevitable, as 'Let Me Roll It' resembles Lennon's inert musicality more than it does McCartney's lively melodicism. McCartney, however, loved it, and with some justification, for like almost every song on the album, it displays a strength and confidence that many found surprising.

McCartney wrote 'Mamunia' while visiting Marrakech with Wings in early 1973. While there, the band stayed at a hotel called Mamounia. The original Arabic meaning of that word – safe haven, or refuge – probably held great significance for McCartney, but rather than take a literal translation, he turned it into a metaphor for rebirth. The first song recorded in Lagos, 'Mamunia' was taped during a heavy tropical storm. (Issued in America as the B-side of 'Jet' (Apple 1871), 'Mamunia' was quickly replaced by 'Let Me Roll It', as there were plans to issue 'Mamunia' as an A-side.

'No Words' was a McCartney-Laine composition, also dating from early 1973. It features all three members of Wings singing unison lead vocals, although Denny and Paul each share a solo spot. It allegedly features roadies Ian Horn and Trevor Jones on backing vocals, but if they are there, they're buried well down in the mix. The basic track was recorded in Lagos, while Tony Visconti's brief orchestration was overdubbed back in London.

While on holiday in Jamaica, the McCartneys had dinner with Dustin Hoffman and his wife. During the evening the subject of songwriting entered the conversation and Hoffman suggested that McCartney might write a song based on Pablo Picasso's last words. As McCartney recalled: "We went back a couple of nights later, and he said, 'I've been thinking about this. I've seen a little article in *Time* magazine about Picasso, and it struck me as being very poetic. I think this would be very good set to music.' So he says there's a little story here. In the article [Picasso] supposedly said, 'Drink to me, drink to my health, you know I can't drink any more.' He went to paint a bit, and then he went to bed at three in the morning. He didn't wake up the next morning and they found him, dead. Dustin Hoffman thought, 'Drink to me, drink to my health, you know I can't drink any more' was a great passing remark. They were Picasso's last words. So he said, 'Could you write something like that?'"

When Wings recorded 'Picasso's Last Words (Drink to Me)', McCartney made a deliberate attempt to echo the artist's visual style with his arrangement. Constructing a collage of themes and melodies, he tried to replicate the painter's fragmented cubist surfaces in musical form. "We thought we'd do this Picasso number, and we thought we'd do it straight," he said. "Then we thought, Picasso was kind of far out in his pictures, he'd done all these different kinds of things, fragmented, cubism, and the whole bit. I thought it would be nice to get a track a bit like that, put it through different moods, cut it up, edit it, mess around with it – like he used to do with his pictures."

Alluding to Picasso's cubist style, Wings extended their usual palette of sonic textures in a brave attempt to emancipate their music from a reliance on hackneyed conventions. McCartney's poetic juxtapositions evoke notions of thematic and temporal simultaneity comparable to the cubist's experiments with form and space. Emphasising structure and texture, McCartney refers us to the process of recording, as Picasso refers the viewer to the process of painting.

The album closes with 'Nineteen Hundred And Eighty Five', a piano-driven rocker with swirling Mellotron, melodic basslines, and a lengthy orchestrated coda. McCartney had the song for some time but couldn't progress any further than the first line. "You see, with a lot of the songs that I do, the first line is it," he said. "It's all in the first line, and then you have to go on and write the second. That's all I had of that song for months. 'No one ever left alive in nineteen hundred and eighty five.'"

Despite its lack of narrative, the song has enough melodic twists and turns to keep the listener engaged until its finale. A mesmerising orchestral climax conveys notions of movement, vitality, and a release of creative energy that echoes the album's extended theme of escape. A brief reprise of 'Band On The Run' neatly bookends the album by returning the listener to the beginning of their flight. By bringing us full circle, McCartney suggests that we are caught in an eternal, inescapable loop of desire and despair. That there is no end is of little importance, it's the journey that's important, not the destination.

US issue rear cover

EMI export edition. Note groove around spindle hole.

Second edition without silver apple at 3 o'clock.

Australian issue

New Zealand issue

Indian issue

Australian re-issue

## Band On The Run data

*Band On The Run* was issued with customised labels with a silver Apple logo at three o'clock, an inner sleeve with lyrics, and a poster of Polaroid photographs taken by Linda in Lagos. The first edition cover has a 'pinched' spine, missing from later editions. EMI also pressed copies of the LP for export. These have textured labels, non-export are smooth, a grooved circle surrounding the spindle hole and the matrix number 'ZYEX-929-3' with 'BLAIRS' hand-etched into the dead wax. The vinyl edition was reissued on its 25th anniversary as a two record set on March 15 1999. This two record set was reissued on November 1 2010 as part of a deal with Concord Music to reissue all McCartney's solo albums as 'deluxe' editions.

In America, Apple/Capitol issued the LP with a slightly altered rear cover, Linda and Denny are swapped, inner sleeve and label similar to the UK edition. Later pressings were issued with Capitol 'Dome' labels. The LP was also issued by Columbia Records with its generic red label.

As important as the music was the cover. It was photographed by Clive Arrowsmith on October 28 1973 and reflects the album's concept of escape and freedom. Paul, Linda, and Denny were joined by a small group of mainly British celebrities, including Michael Parkinson (journalist and talk-show host), Kenny Lynch (singer and actor; he toured with The Beatles in 1963), James Coburn (actor), Clement Freud (politician and raconteur), Christopher Lee (actor), and John Conteh (light heavyweight boxing champion of the world). Arrowsmith took the photograph in the grounds of Osterley Park, west London. The cover shoot was also filmed and later projected behind Wings during their 1975/76 world tour.

Because the cover did not feature the band's name, Capitol manufactured a circular blue sticker with 'PAUL McCARTNEY WINGS' in white, which was adhered to the front cover. A second 2 1/2-inch by 1-inch rectangular sticker with 'INCLUDES THE HITS JET HELEN WHEELS' appeared on later US editions of the LP.

*Band On The Run* became the bestselling album of 1974 in Britain and the seventh bestselling album of the 1970s, just behind Pink Floyd's *Dark Side Of The Moon* and Mike Oldfield's *Tubular Bells*. The album's popularity was confirmed by the number of 'limited' pressings it received in the late 1970s and early 1980s, when coloured vinyl and picture discs became fashionable.

In America, Capitol released a picture disc version (SEAX-11901), also issued in Japan. France issued the LP on yellow vinyl (DC9/C 066 05 503) and in Belgium it was issued on magenta vinyl (5C 062-05503).

Perhaps the rarest pressing was produced by Nimbus Records in 1984. Nimbus are British specialists in audiophile pressings produced to the highest quality. Gerald Reynolds, one of a select handful of Nimbus staff who master the company's 'Supercut' records, confirmed that they always tried to use a studio tape as close to the original as possible. The discs were cut as 'flat' as possible, meaning without any sound manipulation or compression, to ensure that reproduction was as close to the original source tape as possible. The records were pressed on special vinyl, made for Nimbus by ICI, to give a faithful reproduction of the original tape. Nimbus used covers provided by EMI but added a sticker to indicate that they were 'Supercut' pressings.

They made 500 copies of the album initially, which were available exclusively through *Hi Fi Today* magazine. Also, a half-speed mastered edition of the album was issued by Columbia in 1981 (HC 46382).

The album was issued on 8-track cartridge in Britain (8X-PAS 10007) and the USA (8XZ 3415). Capitol also issued a quadraphonic mix on 8-track (Q8W 3415).

Columbia issued *Band On The Run* on CD (CK 36482) on February 29 1984 and Capitol reissued it on December 1 1988 (CDP 7 46055 2). EMI issued the CD in Britain on February 4 1985 and issued a remastered edition (CDPMCOL5) on July 7 1993. A 25th anniversary two-CD edition (4991762) was issued on March 15 1999.

# 1974: Jet to Junior's Farm

'JET' / 'LET ME ROLL IT'
PAUL McCARTNEY AND WINGS
**UK release** February 18 1974; Apple R 5996; chart high No.7.

'JET' / 'MAMUNIA'
**US release** January 28 1974; Apple 1871; withdrawn
'JET' / 'LET ME ROLL IT'
**US release** February 18 1974; Apple 1871; chart high No.1.

'JET'
The days of issuing standalone singles, separate from any album, were rapidly coming to a close. Marketing departments now saw singles as another promotional tool that could substantially improve album sales. Recognising the increased importance of singles and bowing to growing pressure from his record company, McCartney said: "The companies here and in America, worldwide, would like a single on the album. It makes more sense merchandising-wise. But sometimes, I just have to remember that this isn't a record store I'm running; this is supposed to be some kind of art. And if it doesn't fit in, it doesn't fit in." 'Jet' reversed *Band On The Run*'s slow chart descent by sending it back to Number 2 in the British charts and to Number 1 for a further two weeks in the US charts.

**'Jet' data**
'Jet' was issued in Britain with generic Apple labels and paper sleeve. Demonstration copies were manufactured with 'DEMO RECORD NOT FOR SALE' on three lines above the spindle hole and a large 'A' at 2 o'clock. EMI also arranged for contract pressings to be made by Pathe Marconi in France. These records have Apple labels with solid centres and 'Made in France by Pathe Marconi' in addition to the standard perimeter print.

American pressings of the single were issued with two different B-sides and several label variations. The single was initially issued with 'Mamunia' as its B-side and was manufactured with three label variations.

The first has a light green Apple label with 'STEREO' at 9 o'clock and '(from the LP "BAND ON THE RUN" SO-3415') at 10 o'clock; title, composer, and artist credits appear centre bottom in bold print. The second US variant has a dark green Apple label with 'STEREO' at 9 o'clock and the Intro. and Total playing time directly above; song title, composer. and artist credit appear centre bottom in bold print. The third has a dark green Apple label with 'STEREO' at 9 o'clock with the Intro. and Total playing time (incorrectly listed as 2:49) directly above; '(from the LP "BAND ON THE RUN" SO-3415') at 10 o'clock; title, composer, and artist credits centre bottom.

The edition with 'Mamunia' on the B-side was withdrawn, and a new US version issued three weeks later with 'Let Me Roll It' as the flip. A further three label variants were manufactured.

The first has a light green Apple label with 'STEREO' at 9 o'clock but with the Intro. and Total playing time on the right side of the label directly above the catalogue number; song title and artist credit centre bottom in bold print; B-side has the title in bold on two lines at 11 o'clock.

The second variant has a dark green Apple label with identical text layout to the first, but the B-side has the title on one line in thin print. The third variant has a dark green Apple label with 'STEREO' just below 9 o'clock and the Intro. and Total playing time directly above; '(from the LP "BAND ON THE RUN" SO-3415') at 10 o'clock; song title and artist credit centre bottom in thin print; B-side has the title in thin print bottom left on two lines.

American radio stations were issued with demonstration copies of the single (P-1871) featuring a mono edit (A-side) and full-length stereo mix (B-side) of the song. These were issued with light green Apple labels with a black star at 7 o'clock. The song title and artist credit appear centre bottom in bold print.

'Jet' / 'Let Me Roll It' was reissued in the mid 1970s in both Britain and the USA with black and silver Capitol 'dome' labels. Columbia reissued 'Jet' (13-33408) in 1980 as part of its Hall Of Fame series with 'Uncle Albert/Admiral Halsey' on the B-side. This 1980 pressing was issued with red labels; reissued in 1985, it had grey labels.

**'BAND ON THE RUN' / 'ZOO GANG'**
**PAUL McCARTNEY AND WINGS**
**UK release** June 28 1974; Apple R 5997; chart high No.3.

**'BAND ON THE RUN' / 'NINETEEN HUNDRED AND EIGHTY FIVE'**
**PAUL McCARTNEY AND WINGS**
**US release** April 8 1974; Apple 1873; chart high No.1.

### 'Zoo Gang' (McCartney)

Paul McCartney (bass, keyboards), Linda McCartney (keyboards), Denny Laine (guitar), Jimmy McCulloch (guitar), Davy Lutton (drums). Recorded at EMI Odeon Studios, Paris, France. Produced by Paul McCartney.

'BAND ON THE RUN'
With *Band On The Run* still high in the album charts, the title track was released as a single. Another massive hit for McCartney, it reached the Top 5 in Britain and Number 1 in the USA where it also won a Grammy for best pop vocal performance. The single sold over two million copies worldwide – over one million in America alone – and its release ensured that the album at last hit the Number 1 spot in Britain. It also pushed the album back to the top of the American charts for the third time.

'Zoo Gang' was a British ATV television programme produced by Lew Grade, who asked McCartney to write the show's theme tune. After completing *Band On The Run* in December 1973, Paul, Linda and Denny, along with Davy Lutton (drums) and Jimmy McCulloch (guitar), visited Paris, primarily to work on some of Linda's songs. While there, they also recorded 'Zoo Gang', as McCartney put it: "Just to see how it'd feel playing with musicians on a loose no-strings-attached basis". 'Zoo Gang' was a product of these 'test' sessions and found its way onto the B-side of 'Band On The Run'.

In an attempt to benefit from the publicity created by the television series, 'Zoo Gang' was also recorded by a group of session musicians, Jungle Juice, and issued on May 25 1974 by Bradley Records (BRAD 7407). The group, which included Colin Frechter on keyboards, recorded a similar-sounding instrumental, 'Monkey Business', for the B-side. Both sides of the record were produced by Tony Hiller, who did such a good job at recreating Wings' original that it fooled many into believing that Jungle Juice was another of McCartney's pseudonyms. In fact, neither McCartney nor Wings had anything to do with the Jungle Juice single.

## 'Band On The Run' data

The US pressing (Apple 1873) was backed with 'Nineteen Hundred And Eighty Five' rather than 'Zoo Gang' and was manufactured with three label variations. The first has a dark green Apple label with 'STEREO' at 9 o'clock and the Intro. and Total playing time directly below; '(from the LP "BAND ON THE RUN" SO-3415') at 10 o'clock; song title, composer, and band credits bottom centre in bold. The second variant has a dark green Apple label with 'STEREO' at 9 o'clock; '(from the LP "BAND ON THE RUN" SO-3415') at 10 o'clock; song title and composer credit top centre; band name bottom centre. The third US variant has a light green Apple label with 'STEREO' at 9 o'clock and the catalogue number directly below; '(from the LP "BAND ON THE RUN" SO-3415') at 10 o'clock; song title, composer, and band name bottom centre; Intro. time on the right side of the label above 'Total-5:09'.

In Britain, Apple issued two demonstration singles. The first has edited and full-length versions of the A-side and white-labels with the EMI box logo top centre and 'DEMO RECORD NOT FOR SALE' above the spindle hole. The second, PSR 359, also with white-labels, is backed with 'Let Me Roll It' and has 'FROM THE ALBUM "BAND ON THE RUN" PAS10007' on three lines top centre. Two demonstration singles were issued to American radio stations. The first (P-1873) was issued with a mono edit on the A-side and the full-length stereo version on the B-side. The second (PRO 6825) was issued with mono and stereo edits of the A-side on either side of the record. These were issued with light green Apple labels with a black star at 7 o'clock and the song title, composer, and band name centre bottom in bold.

Reissued in the mid 1970s, 'Band On The Run' was manufactured in Britain and America with black and silver Capitol 'dome' labels. 'Band On The Run' was reissued by Columbia (13-33409) in 1980 as part of its Hall Of Fame series with 'Helen Wheels' on the B-side. The 1980 pressing was issued with red labels; the 1985 re-pressing with grey labels.

## 'WALKING IN THE PARK WITH ELOISE' / 'BRIDGE OVER THE RIVER SUITE'
## THE COUNTRY HAMS

**UK release** October 18 1974; EMI EMI 2220; failed to chart.
**US release** December 2 1974; EMI EMI 3977; failed to chart.

### 'Walking In The Park With Eloise' (James McCartney Senior)
Paul McCartney (bass), Chet Atkins (guitar), Floyd Cramer (piano), Geoff Britton (drums), Denis Good, Bobby Thompson, Bill Puitt (saxophones), Don Sheffield (trumpet). Recorded at Sound Shop Studios, Nashville, TN, USA.

### 'Bridge Over The River Suite' (McCartney)
Paul McCartney (bass, washboard), Linda McCartney (keyboards), Jimmy McCulloch (guitar), Denny Laine (guitar), Davy Lutton (drums), Bill Puitt (saxophone), George Tidwell, Barry McDonald (trumpets), Norman Ray (baritone saxophone), Dale Quillen (trombone), Thaddeus Richard (saxophone). Recorded at EMI Odeon Studios, Paris, France and Sound Shop Studios, Nashville. Both produced by Paul McCartney.

'WALKING IN THE PARK WITH ELOISE'
Having completed *Band On The Run*, McCartney started to look for replacements for drummer Denny Seiwell and guitarist Henry McCullough. Drummer Davy Lutton was employed as a temporary stand-in as was guitarist Jimmy McCulloch, both recorded with Wings at EMI Odeon Studios, Paris, in late 1973. McCartney had had his eye on McCulloch since spotting him in Thunderclap Newman in 1969. "He looked good and he's got a great wrist," McCartney enthused. "When he hit's a chord it really rings." Having worked with several bands including John Mayall's band and Stone The Crows he was looking for something more stable, and Wings would eventually offer him that option. As he explained: "I'm sick and tired of being in and out of bands. I want to get something down on record that's going to be appreciated instead of always being in new bands that so few people hear."

However, McCartney wanted to keep the band line-up fluid and McCulloch would be with Wings for the best part of nine months before it was officially announced that he was a full-time member. "It was quite strange at the time," he said, "I just thought I was just doing the sessions. And in Paris they'd just finished *Band On The Run* and they had a couple of Linda's songs. Turned out really well. We jammed a lot and got on really well."

Finding a drummer was going to be a little more difficult and so McCartney held auditions for Seiwell's replacement at the Albery Theatre in London beginning on April 26 1974. Competition for the job was fierce with around 50 drummers auditioning. Waiting in the wings that day was Geoff Britton. He was eager to play with his hero but left disappointed. Paul, Linda and Denny didn't play that day but sat out front while a surrogate band stood in for them.

Britton recalled: "I was a bit disappointed, actually, because I thought it would be a chance to play with McCartney, but they hired session men instead. I wasn't really nervous, although I might've been a bit apprehensive. We had to play about four numbers – some of it quite advanced stuff for an ordinary rock'n'roll drummer. Anyway, I got up there and did my stuff. A few days later I got this phone call and they said I was on the shortlist of five, and this time it would be Paul and the group playing. That time I had a 20 percent chance, yet I felt it was more hopeless than ever."

Britton needn't have worried, his no nonsense style to drumming was just what McCartney wanted. Left with a choice between Roger Pope, who joined Elton John's band, or Britton he went with the latter. "I didn't want a drummer who plays a lot of fills," McCartney recalled. "For the lack of a better word. I like 'spade' drumming. A real simple beat and they hold it like a metronome and occasionally put in some funky things."

With Britton on board, the band headed to Nashville to get to know one another and rehearse. In June and July 1974, during a six-week stay in Nashville, McCartney wrote some new songs, rehearsed the new line-up, and recorded 'Junior's Farm' and an instrumental, 'Walking In The Park with Eloise', written by his father. As Linda recalled, the recording came about almost by accident. "We were having dinner with Chet Atkins, the guitar player, one night in Nashville, and Paul had been playing a lot of his music for Chet, and he said: 'Here's one that my dad wrote a long time ago' – and he started playing it. Chet got talking to Paul, saying that the song should be recorded and that it would be nice for his dad. So we got Chet playing on it and Floyd Cramer, the piano player, and Chet got together a nice little band called The Country Hams with lots of other Nashville people."

McCartney said that his father was thrilled with his debut single. "He loved having a record out – but he's very shy ... and he didn't like all the publicity. I remember him being very emotional about it when I first played it to him. He said I really shouldn't have bothered, but I know he enjoyed it."

While McCartney was recording 'Country Dreamer' (B-side of 'Helen Wheels'; see October 1973) he improvised a melody that formed the basis of 'Bridge Over The River Suite'. Recorded with drummer Davy Lutton and guitarist Jimmy McCulloch at EMI's Paris studio in December 1973, it's untypical of Wings, although the introduction recalls 'Let Me Roll It' from the previous year. The brass section, scored by Paul and Tony Dorsey, was overdubbed in Nashville in July 1974.

### 'Walking In The Park With Eloise' data
The single was issued in Britain and the USA with generic EMI labels and picture sleeve. In America, EMI issued a mono/stereo demonstration single P-3997 (PRO-6993). In Britain, EMI issued demonstration copies with 'DEMO RECORD NOT FOR RESALE' on two lines below the spindle hole and an 'A' above the A-side label's spindle hole.

114

## 'JUNIOR'S FARM' / 'SALLY G'
## PAUL McCARTNEY AND WINGS
**UK release** October 25 1974; Apple R 5999; chart high No.16.
**US release** November 4 1974; Apple 1875; chart high No.3.

### 'Junior's Farm' (McCartney)
Paul McCartney (bass, vocals), Linda McCartney (keyboards, vocals), Denny Laine (guitar, vocals), Jimmy McCulloch (guitar), Geoff Britton (drums).
### 'Sally G' (McCartney)
Paul McCartney (bass, guitar, vocals), Linda McCartney (backing vocals), Denny Laine (guitar), Jimmy McCulloch (guitar), Geoff Britton (drums), Vassar Clements (fiddle), Buddy Emmons (pedal steel guitar), Johnny Gimble (fiddle).
Both recorded at Sound Shop Studios, Nashville, TN, USA. Both mixed at Abbey Road Studios, London, England. Both produced by Paul McCartney.

### 'JUNIOR'S FARM'
What little recording Wings did in Nashville went relatively smoothly, but relations within the band remained tense. As early as August 1974, only weeks after the group's return to Britain, the *NME* carried the headline "Wings Upheaval". Problems revolved around money and contracts, as Laine explained. "We went to Nashville with the idea that we'd get this group together and we'd all sign contracts and be Wings, as a business thing. But then it seemed as if it was being a bit rushed. I thought, 'Hang on – let's make sure that this is the right group.' Then I started thinking about contracts, and I decided that I could be in any group without signing a contract. It just didn't seem necessary to me, and the minute I said this to Paul he said, 'Great, that's the way I want it too,' and then I realised that we were only going through this thing because we'd all been advised to do it. It wasn't what we wanted."

In an attempt to paper over the cracks, MPL issued a statement that only added to the confusion. (MPL is McCartney Productions Ltd, an umbrella company founded in 1971 by McCartney for his management and business interests.) Failing to confirm the band's status, the statement simply said: "Wings members are free to pursue their own musical careers. This will enable them to develop working relations free of contractual ties. In future Wings will have a fluid concept, which will be adapted to suit current and future projects." Disputes over contracts and money had contributed to McCullough and Seiwell's departure and would beleaguer Wings throughout the 1970s. Consequently, the concept of fluidity quickly became a reality, with various individuals joining and leaving the McCartney–Laine–McCartney core over the next few years.

'Junior's Farm' was recorded in Nashville and was partly inspired by Junior 'Curley' Putman, owner of the ranch near Lebanon, Nashville, where Wings were living and rehearsing. Bob Dylan's 'Maggie's Farm' provided further inspiration, as McCartney recalled. "To me, in a way, it was a bit reminiscent of Dylan's thing, 'ain't gonna work on Maggie's farm any more'. So the idea [was] we'll have another farm, rather than Maggie's farm. And so the idea was to just get a fantasy song about this person Junior – and we recorded it in Nashville with Jimmy McCulloch on guitar and Geoff Britton on drums. Jimmy played a really nice solo; we had a good session on that one." Thus Wings Mk.4 were born: Paul, Linda, and Laine plus McCulloch and Britton.

'Junior's Farm' was a blistering rocker that matched earlier examples like 'Hi, Hi, Hi' in ferocity and energy. McCartney was concerned that Lennon had stolen his thunder as a rocker and was working hard to regain the title as The Beatle that rocked. "I don't like [it] when I keep attempting rock things [and] you get 'That's another nice soft rock from Paul… another nice light rocker', I don't like that at all," he told the *Melody Maker*. 'Junior's Farm' was a classic McCartney rocker through and through. McCartney might have been tarred a balladeer but his fears were unfounded. When he wanted to he could rock as hard as the next, he just needed the occasional poke from Lennon or contemporaries like The Who to get the creative juices flowing.

'Sally G' was also written and recorded during the Nashville sojourn. It's a country-flavoured ballad, originally called 'Diane' after the singer Diane Gaffney. McCartney changed the title to 'Sally G' upon learning that Gaffney was suing a newspaper after her name had appeared in it without her permission. Explaining the song's genesis, he said: "When I'm in a place, it's not uncommon for me to want to write about where I am. Elton John did 'Philadelphia Freedom', you know? You see a lot of that: someone will turn up and write a song the next day."

While in Nashville, McCartney was taken to Printers Alley and spent some time in a bar called Skull's Rainbow Room. "There was a few people just playing country music," he said, "and we imagined a bit more than we had seen for 'Sally G'. I didn't see anyone named Sally G when I was in Printers Alley, nor did I see anyone who ran her eyes over me when she was singing 'a tangled mime'. That was my imagination adding something to it, the reality of it."

### 'Junior's Farm' data

In Britain, EMI subcontracted an unidentified manufacturer, possibly Decca, to press copies of the single. The subcontracted pressings can be identified by their heavier weight, wider clearance between the push-out centre and the record, and the handwritten matrix number (7YCE21751 - 3). Two versions of the demonstration single were issued. The first had an edited version of 'Junior's Farm' on the A-side and a full-length version on the B-side. The second has reversed A and B-sides with the full-length version of 'Sally G' on the A-side.

Four label variants were issued in the USA. The first has a light green Apple label with 'STEREO' at 10 o'clock; Intro. and Total playing time at 3 o'clock; song title, writing credit, and band name bottom centre; 'Recorded in England' (although the single was, of course, recorded in America) at 11 o'clock. The second has identical text layout to the first but 'All rights reserved' etc. is on five lines below the catalogue number. The third variant has a dark green Apple label with 'STEREO' at 10 o'clock; catalogue number at 9 o'clock; 'Recorded in England' at 8 o'clock; song title, writing credit, and band name bottom centre. The fourth US variant has a dark green Apple label with 'STEREO' at 10 o'clock; Intro. and Total playing time at 9 o'clock; song title, writing credit, band name, and 'Recorded in England' bottom centre.

In America, demonstration copies of both the A and B-side were issued with light green Apple labels with a black star at 7 o'clock. 'Junior's Farm' (P-1875 [PRO-6999]) was issued with a mono edit on the A-side and the full-length stereo version on the B-side. An alternative edit that removed the second verse was prepared for American radio stations and issued as a 7-inch single (SPRO-8003) with white labels. 'Sally G' (P-1875 [PRO-8000]) was presented in-full in mono on the A-side and stereo on the B-side. The single was reissued in both Britain and the USA in the mid 1970s with black and silver Capitol 'dome' labels.

Decca contract pressing

# 1975: Sally G to Venus And Mars / Rock Show

## 'SALLY G' / 'JUNIOR'S FARM'
## PAUL McCARTNEY AND WINGS
**UK release** February 7 1975; Apple R 5999; failed to re-enter chart.
**US release** December 24 1974; Apple 1875; chart high No.17.

### 'SALLY G'
Although McCartney had resisted lifting singles from albums to avoid accusations that he was milking a cash cow, he'd been persuaded to issue several singles from *Band On The Run* and was obviously impressed with the difference it made to sales. Putting a single out was a good way of keeping the band in the public eye. So why not take the idea a stage further and simply flip 'A' and 'B' sides? "That was the whole point about 'Sally G'", McCartney told *Melody Maker*. "We flipped that and I thought it might seem like we're trying to fool the public. But it isn't, it's only to get a bit of exposure on that song. Otherwise it just dies a death, and only the people who bought 'Junior's Farm' get to hear 'Sally G'. That's what I'm making records for. It's not for the bread, although I like that too, it's just that if you do something in my particular field, you want people to hear it."

Issued as a demonstration single on both sides of the Atlantic, 'Sally G' was distributed to radio stations in an attempt to generate airplay and, it was hoped, to extend the single's chart run. Although Wings had recently recorded in Nashville and had commenced recording what would become the *Venus And Mars* album, there was little new material available to fill the gap between albums. Although the band had remained busy throughout 1974, much of what they recorded was either for other artists, such as McCartney's brother, or was not intended for commercial release.

So 'Junior's Farm' / 'Sally G' was flipped to exploit the lucrative country market. This worked in America, where country music was considerably more popular, and 'Sally G' reached Number 17 in the American charts in early 1975. However, in Britain this marketing ploy flopped.

**PAUL McCARTNEY AND WINGS HAVE A TWO-SIDED SMASH HIT!**

**SALLY G** (1875)
is the hit single on the other side of the hit single

**JUNIOR'S FARM**
is the hit single on the other side of the hit single

American demonstration copies of the single were issued with a mono A-side and stereo B-side. British demonstration copies replicate the commercial single but with A- and B-sides flipped and 'DEMO RECORD NOT FOR SALE' on three lines above the spindle hole, a large 'A' at four o'clock and the date '(7.2.75)' below the spindle hole.

'LISTEN TO WHAT THE MAN SAID' / 'LOVE IN SONG'
WINGS
**UK release** May 16 1975; Capitol R 6006; chart high No.6.
**US release** May 26 1975; Capitol 4091; chart high No.1.

### 'Listen To What The Man Said' (McCartney)
Paul McCartney (bass, piano, vocals), Linda McCartney (keyboards, backing vocals), Denny Laine (guitar, backing vocals), Jimmy McCulloch (guitar), Joe English (drums), Tom Scott (saxophone), Dave Mason (guitar). Recorded at Sea Saint Studios, New Orleans, LA, USA, and Wally Heider, Los Angeles, CA, USA.
### 'Love In Song' (McCartney)
Paul McCartney (guitar, upright bass, vocals), Linda McCartney (backing vocals), Denny Laine (guitar), Jimmy McCulloch (guitar), Geoff Britton (drums). Recorded at Abbey Road Studios, London, England.

'LISTEN TO WHAT THE MAN SAID'
Wings began recording *Venus And Mars* in London before moving to New Orleans where they cut 'Listen To What The Man Said'. Recording at EMI's Abbey Road Studios, the group had only managed to complete three songs to McCartney's satisfaction. But if McCartney thought that the relaxed atmosphere of New Orleans would make the process any easier he was wrong. No sooner had they unpacked their bags and settled into a recording routine than Geoff Brittan downed sticks and returned to London.

Whatever was happening backstage was affecting an already delicate social balance. Although the line-up had been rehearsing and recording for some months, MPL didn't officially announce the arrival of Geoff Britton and Jimmy McCulloch until November 1974. McCulloch had been under contract to Robert Stigwood and therefore unable to sign with MPL. "I've really been with Wings for about nine months but it wasn't announced before probably because they anticipated hassles. But now Wings have decided to drop all that contract business," he told the *NME*. Although he was officially tied to Stigwood's organisation, McCulloch let slip that he'd been put on a retainer by MPL for three months but that under the new agreement he would only be paid when Wings were rehearsing, recording or performing. In other words, the MPL statement that members of Wings were "free to pursue their own musical careers... free of contractual ties" was entirely accurate.

Speaking to the same paper Britton said: "There was talk of contracts in the beginning, but we decided it was better if nothing was contracted. If you're a real pro and you've got a tour booked, you don't phone up and say, 'I'm not coming.' That's just not on." Despite his apparent commitment to the group, Britton wouldn't be with the group much longer. Clashes with McCulloch and personal problems came to a head in New Orleans. "I was in the States and we were starting work on *Venus And Mars*, and my wife started talking about separation and divorce. I came home to sort it out," he said. Because he didn't have a contract, Britton was free to walk, which is exactly what he did.

Tony Dorsey, who was arranging the horn parts, recommended Joe English. "I was rehearsing with Bonnie Bramlett (of Delaney and Bonnie), and I was thinking of going on the road with her band when I received a call from Paul in New Orleans asking me to play on the album," recalled English. "Fortunately, I was able to find Bonnie a replacement drummer pretty quickly, and there were no hang ups as far as she was concerned." Booked as a temporary stand-in, he so impressed McCartney that he asked him to join full-time while the group were mixing the album in Los Angeles.

With or without a new drummer, attempts to record 'Listen To What The Man Said' didn't go smoothly, as McCartney recalled. "It was one of the songs we'd gone in with high hopes for. Whenever I would play it on the piano, people would say, 'Oh I like that one.' But when we did the backing track, we thought we really didn't get it together at all." In an attempt to save the track, McCartney asked Dave Mason to overdub some guitar parts, but the problem of what to do for a solo remained. As luck would have it, Tom Scott, a respected saxophonist, provided the solution. McCartney: "We said ... give him a ring, see if he turns up – and he turned up within half an hour. There he was, with his sax, and he sat down in the studio playing through." Improvising to the Wings backing track, Scott delivered an exceptional solo that transformed a good song into something extraordinary. His first take was the best, but as McCartney said: "No one could believe it, so we went out and tried a few more, but they weren't as good. I think what he plays on that song is lovely and that, overall, it worked."

A slice of radio-friendly pop, 'Listen To What The Man Said' was the ideal vehicle with which to introduce the new Wings line-up. It's a joyous celebration of love and life, buoyed by Linda's equally exuberant backing vocals, a sign of her growing confidence. Lifting the spirits like a glimpse of blue sky on a cloudy day, the song gave the band its first Top 10 single since 'Band On The Run'.

The B-side, 'Love In Song', was recorded at Abbey Road in late 1974 and offers yet another reworking of McCartney's favourite theme, love. He wrote the song on a 12-string acoustic guitar, and suggested that it just came to him. "I feel I don't have a lot of control over some songs, but some songs I do. But with this song I just started playing my guitar, singing those words, wrote them down, and I said to Linda, 'How do you like that?' And that was it." The measured arrangement and melancholic lyric suggest a slight distancing of its author from his subject, but the warmth of McCartney's vocal more than compensates for the song's reserved tone.

### 'Listen To What The Man Said' data
This was Wings' first single for Capitol. Or was it? McCartney and the other ex-Beatles were still signed to EMI/Capitol but thus far had issued their solo releases under the Apple Records imprint, even though they were really EMI/Parlophone/Capitol releases. McCartney's contract with EMI didn't expire until January 1976, but for some reason he elected to release this record and the *Venus And Mars* album on the Capitol Records imprint, his US label. However, Apple Records issued 'Listen To What The Man Said' by in Portugal (8E 006-96638), 'Letting Go' in Italy (3C 006 96940), and the *Venus And Mars* LP in Uruguay (SAPL 30.535) so McCartney's liaison with the company he'd helped form wasn't quite over. (Capitol issued mono/stereo edits to American radio stations of the 'Listen' A-side as a demonstration single (PRO-8183).)

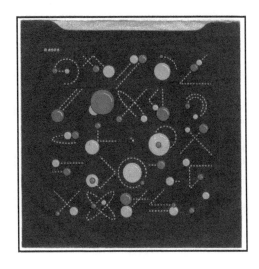

US curve top picture sleeve

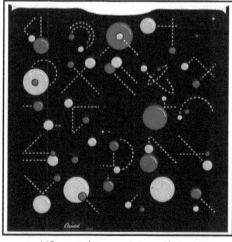

US straight top picture sleeve

*VENUS AND MARS*
WINGS
**Side 1** 'Venus And Mars', 'Rock Show', 'Love In Song', 'You Gave Me The Answer', 'Magneto And Titanium Man', 'Letting Go'.
**Side 2** 'Venus And Mars (reprise)', 'Spirits Of Ancient Egypt', 'Medicine Jar', 'Call Me Back Again', 'Listen To What The Man Said', 'Treat Her Gently – Lonely Old People', 'Crossroads'.
**UK release** May 30 1975; LP Capitol PCTC 254; 8-track cartridge Capitol 8X-PCTC 254 released May 1975; chart high No.1.
**US release** May 27 1975; LP Capitol SMAS-11419; 8-track cartridge Capitol 8XT-11419; quadraphonic 8-track cartridge Capitol Q8W-11419; chart high No.1.

**'Venus And Mars'** (McCartney)
Paul McCartney (bass, vocals), Linda McCartney (keyboards, backing vocals), Denny Laine (guitar, backing vocals), Jimmy McCulloch (guitar), Joe English (drums).
**'Rock Show'** (McCartney)
Personnel as 'Venus And Mars' except add Allen Toussaint (piano).
**'Love In Song'** (McCartney)
Paul McCartney (guitar, upright bass, vocals), Linda McCartney (backing vocals), Denny Laine (guitar), Jimmy McCulloch (guitar), Geoff Britton (drums).
**'You Gave Me The Answer'** (McCartney)
Paul McCartney (piano, vocals), Linda McCartney (keyboards, backing vocals), Denny Laine (bass, backing vocals), Jimmy McCulloch (guitar), Joe English (drums).
**'Magneto And Titanium Man'** (McCartney)
Personnel as 'Venus And Mars'.
**'Letting Go'** (McCartney)
Personnel as 'Venus And Mars'.
**'Spirits Of Ancient Egypt'** (McCartney)
Paul McCartney (bass, backing vocals), Linda McCartney (keyboards, backing vocals), Denny Laine (guitar, vocals), Jimmy McCulloch (guitar), Joe English (drums).
**'Medicine Jar'** (McCulloch, Allen)
Paul McCartney (bass, backing vocals), Linda McCartney (keyboards, backing vocals), Denny Laine (guitar, backing vocals), Jimmy McCulloch (guitar, vocals), Joe English (drums).
**'Call Me Back Again'** (McCartney)
Paul McCartney (bass, piano, vocals), Linda McCartney (keyboards, backing vocals), Denny Laine (guitar, backing vocals), Jimmy McCulloch (guitar), Joe English (drums).
**'Treat Her Gently – Lonely Old People'** (McCartney)
Personnel as 'Call Me Back Again'.
**'Crossroads'** (Hatch)
Paul McCartney (piano, bass), Linda McCartney (keyboards), Denny Laine (guitar), Jimmy McCulloch (guitar), Joe English (drums). All recorded at Sea Saint Studios, New Orleans, LA, USA and Wally Heider, Los Angeles, CA, USA, except 'Letting Go' recorded at Abbey Road Studios, London, England, and Sea Saint Studios, New Orleans, LA, USA. All produced by Paul McCartney.

## VENUS AND MARS

Another album, another line-up. Despite personnel changes, Wings were on a roll and the Mk.5 line-up – Paul, Linda, Laine, and McCulloch with the addition of Joe English on drums – sounded confident and mature. But although the album benefits from an assured and sophisticated approach to record making, it was hampered by too many run-of-the-mill songs. More stylistically diverse than its predecessor, *Venus And Mars* reflects McCartney's musical tastes, influences and his delight in genre-hopping. However, his mix-and-match approach to compiling the album, which found rough-house rockers juxtaposed with twee ballads, did little to bolster his standing with his critics. Writing in the *NME*, Charles Shaar Murray considered the album "one of the worst albums I've ever heard from a so-called 'Major' artist." He continued "Venus And Mars is a symptom of decadence because it is the product of a considerable talent in an advanced state of decay." However, Greg Shaw, writing in *Phonograph Record*, thought the album "Paul's most advanced, refined, diverse effort yet, and should allay the fears of those who suspected that after one good album he might go back to nursery rhymes or one of the other forms of mediocrity of which he's proven more than capable in the past." Whatever the critics thought, the public liked it enough to send it to the top of the charts on both sides of the Atlantic.

Sessions for *Venus And Mars* began at Abbey Road in late 1974, with Geoff Britton occupying the drummer's stool. 'Love In Song', 'Letting Go' and 'Medicine Jar' were completed, along with an early attempt at 'Rock Show'. However, McCartney abandoned 'Rock Show' after ten days in the studio simply because it wasn't working. Speaking to *Melody Maker*, he said: "It's an attempt at a kind of rocking thing. The type that you've got to get right. I don't like this when I keep attempting rock things [and] you get 'That's another nice soft rocker from Paul…another nice light rocker, I don't like all that." Wings first attempt at 'Rock Show' was considerably longer than the remake but lacked focus. Part of the problem might have been that the band were improvising too much and like 'Soily' McCartney had yet to come up with the right arrangement.

Abandoning London for Jamaica, McCartney spent his vacation programming the album. "We'd been in Jamaica before we went to New Orleans and for the first time ever, I'd got all the songs together. I wrote it all out and stuck it all together like a scroll that went from here to the end of the room. So I had that all together and we just turned up and started recording." Then, in January 1975, Wings relocated to Sea Saint Studios in New Orleans. The change of location wasn't as inspiring as Lagos, but according to McCartney it had an affect on the music. "I think it always rubs off a bit, just in the kind of arrangement and who's there. There's a couple of tunes we've go brass on and it's New Orleans brass. But the album doesn't sound very New Orleansy to me. We just wanted to record in America and find a musical city."

Settling into a relaxed routine the band recorded from late afternoon to early morning. The first song they recorded, 'Lunch Box/Odd Sox', failed to make the album (it was eventually issued in 1980 as the B-side to 'Coming Up'). Work continued on the album for several weeks before the band took a short break in early February to enjoy the Mardi Gras. After a five-day break, recording resumed on Ash Wednesday with 'My Carnival'. This song also failed to make the album and was eventually issued on the B-side of 'Spies Like Us' in 1985. It was around this time that Geoff Britton quit the band and his replacement, Joe English, joined. With the basic tracks completed,

Wings moved to Wally Heider Studios, Los Angeles, to add overdubs, backing vocals, and strings, the latter supervised by Sid Sharpe.

Their stay in Los Angeles coincided with the annual Grammy awards, at which Paul and Linda received an award for *Band On The Run*. The day after the ceremony, McCartney was driving Linda and the children back to their rented house in Malibu when he failed to stop at a red traffic light and was pulled over by a highway patrol man. On stopping the car, the officer claimed he smelt a strong aroma of marijuana; he later claimed to have found a lit joint on the floor of the car along with a quantity of the drug.

The McCartneys were arrested, but when Linda insisted that the marijuana belonged to her, Paul was allowed to drive the children home. Linda probably took the rap because she was an American citizen and Paul, already finding it hard to get work permits for the USA, would have found it even harder had he been found guilty of possession of an illegal substance. Had he been convicted, it's unlikely that the American authorities would have granted further work permits, and the proposed American tour would have been cancelled. Found guilty of possessing marijuana, Linda was offered psychiatric treatment and ordered to attend six sessions with a psychiatrist to overcome her problem. The charges were later dismissed as Linda had completed a six-month course in Britain on the dangers of drugs.

On their return to Britain, Wings undertook four months of rehearsals in preparation for what was to become their most technically complex and extensive tour – it covered ten countries during a 13-month period – and also the most successful. Wings Mk.5 gave their first official live performance in front of an invited audience at Studio 5, Elstree, to the north-west of London, on September 6 1975 (though they had earlier jammed with The Meters aboard a converted riverboat in the USA). The Elstree performance took place three days before the first date of their British tour, which commenced in Southampton. This concert, along with several others, notably Newcastle, Liverpool, and Glasgow, were recorded and filmed for future use, but remain unseen (the footage was later superseded by film of the American tour, which was used for *Rock Show*).

### Venus And Mars songs
At the time, many suspected that the Venus and Mars of the album's title track referred to Paul and Linda. But as McCartney explained, this couldn't have been further from the truth. "When we had a party in the States to celebrate having finished the album, someone came up to us and said, 'Hello Venus. Hello Mars.' I thought, 'Oh no.' When I write songs, I'm not necessarily talking about me, although a psychoanalyst would say, 'Yes you are mate.' But as far as I'm concerned, I'm not."

McCartney was unaware that Venus and Mars held any symbolic meaning – in Greek mythology Venus is the god of love and Mars the god of war – or that the two planets are adjacent to one another. Those looking for any allegorical meaning in the title of the album and its opening track were disappointed. McCartney made it clear that the song had nothing to do with himself or Linda. "[It] is about an imaginary friend who's got a girlfriend who's the kind of person who asks you what your sign is before they say hello. That's it: 'a good friend of mine studies the stars.' In fact, in the first verse it's 'a good friend of mine *follows* the stars,' so it could be ambiguous: a groupie or an astrologer."

A lengthy coda segues 'Venus And Mars' with the best up-tempo song on the album, 'Rock Show'. It was written with the forthcoming world tour in mind, around references to venues that the band had played or which happened to provide a suitable rhyme. "I start off with an idea," explained McCartney. "Rock Show, boom! Concertgebouw came into my mind, because that's one of the places you play in Amsterdam. We played there, so I rhymed it with 'Rock Show' in an English pronunciation of gebouw. 'Long hair,' well, where else? Madison Square. 'Rock and Roll,' well, that rhymes with Hollywood Bowl. Often these things that turn out to be great afterwards are just searches for a rhyme. I could see how you may think, well, he's doing this, but for me it's just writing a song."

McCartney wrote 'You Gave Me The Answer' as an affectionate homage to the golden age of the Hollywood musical, inspired by childhood memories of listening to the BBC Home Service and his father playing the piano. "When I started to listen to music, the kind of music was Fred Astaire and *The Billy Cotton Band Show*, Cole Porter's type of lyrics," he said. "I like the Fred Astaire films … I think, wow, great, boy, can they dance! Boy, can they arrange tunes. They were only doing what we're doing now, but some of the time they were much better at it."

In an era of heavy metal and glam-rock, McCartney's decision to rework a dead style seemed as anachronistic as the monochrome stock on which Astaire's movies were made. Nevertheless, 'You Gave Me The Answer' shouldn't have come as a surprise, for as George Martin noted: "Paul always had that sneaking regard for the old rooty-tooty music." Far from a radical departure, the piece continues where 'When I'm Sixty Four', 'Honey Pie', or 'Walking In The Park With Eloise' had left off.

McCartney wrote 'Magneto And Titanium Man' while on holiday in Jamaica. He remembered: "We'd go into the supermarket every Saturday, when they got a new stock of comics in. I didn't use to read comics from 11 onwards, I thought I'd grown out of them, but I came back to them a couple of years ago. I think it's very clever how they do it. I love the names; I love the whole comic book thing." Just as Lennon had taken the lyrics for 'Being For The Benefit Of Mr Kite' from a Victorian poster, so McCartney took his inspiration from a Marvel comic book. Apparently it's a song about heroes and villains; closer inspection reveals a subtext concerning a personal relationship, albeit a fictitious one.

He explores relationships of a more personal kind in 'Letting Go'. Like many of McCartney's songs, it's about Linda: her potential and inner beauty. It also marks a moment of catharsis that sees McCartney symbolically offer Linda her independence. But this is limited autonomy and comes at a price. The cost? Celebrity, something Linda abhorred. McCartney's lyric implies that Linda's independence can only be assured by her participation in his world (showbusiness), which means she must distance herself from hers (home and family).

Inspired by a book about the Great Pyramids, McCartney wrote 'Spirits Of Ancient Egypt'. A pedestrian rocker, it was saved by a lyric as surreal as a Dali painting. McCartney let Denny Laine take the lead vocal, suggesting, perhaps, that he was not enamoured with the song. However, it was performed throughout Wings 1975/'76 world tour, and a live recording with an extended guitar solo was programmed for *Wings Over America*.

McCulloch wrote 'Medicine Jar' while with Stone The Crows and introduced it to Wings while they rehearsed in Nashville. "I had been writing for a while. I'd done about five songs for the next Crows album before they split," he said. "Actually I've just done one with Paul now called 'Medicine Jar', it's an anti-drug song. It'll probably be on the next album. But I don't write much." 'Medicine Jar' turned out to be sadly prophetic. With hindsight, all the signs of McCulloch's drink and drug abuse were evident. Speaking some years after McCulloch's death, McCartney said: "Jimmy ... was an erratic personality, if you want to put it nicely. Jimmy wanted it all and he wanted it now. He'd come in off the piss at four in the morning and he'd put his stereo on loud and he was out of it. If anything – looking from now, the perspective now – it's lucky we ever held the group together."

Inspired by their surroundings, Paul and Linda both wrote songs about New Orleans, notably 'My Carnival' and 'New Orleans'. (Linda's 'New Orleans' appeared on her posthumous solo album, *Wide Prairie*, in 1998.) While not referring specifically to the city, 'Call Me Back Again' was written during a stay at the Beverly Hills Hotel in 1974 and nevertheless bears traces of its influence.

Tight and sassy, it blends several influences into a musical cocktail that is as intoxicating as New Orleans itself. McCartney finished the lyrics while in the city and had Tony Dorsey write the brass arrangement. Influenced by some of New Orleans' finest soul singers, McCartney delivered a killer vocal that underlines a recording to relish. "I ended up just sort of ad libbing a bit," he said, "stretching out a bit. I like that myself. I had a chance to sing." Partly improvised, his vocal has a depth of emotion rarely equalled and reveals what a supreme vocalist he is.

'Treat Her Gently – Lonely Old People' was written in two parts, but unlike previous songs it wasn't completed by welding two unfinished fragments together. Rather, the second theme emerged from the first. McCartney: "I wrote the 'Treat Her Gently' bit as it fell into the key of D, and once I was in D I thought, 'Well, how do I get out of this?' And so I wrote the second half of the thing. It just fell together. They just fell into each other, and I wrote it as I was practising the other, almost."

Evoking what can be the melancholia of old age, McCartney's acute observation conveys the sense of loneliness many experience as they wait out their years in drab nursing homes in dull seaside towns. An essay in mental and physical disintegration, it's haunted by the ghost of Eleanor Rigby but sidesteps the finality of the former in favour of a secular purgatory, consisting of endless visits to the park and the monotony of daytime television. His lyric reveals what awaits us all, but, unlike the bleak 'Eleanor Rigby', 'Treat Her Gently – Lonely Old People' has real compassion and points to the pleasures of companionship and love, even if it is set in a bleak urban landscape.

*Venus And Mars* closes with a version of 'Crossroads', the theme tune to a mundane British TV soap opera. Outside of the UK, the tune meant little, as McCartney admitted when he was interviewed for the *NME*. "This fellow who was helping me [Tony Dorsey] thought it was a lovely tune. He thought I'd written it. He thought it was just a beautiful little tune, and it is." He chose to close the album with Crossroads because "it's a bit of a British joke, but I'd still like to put it out. If you don't get the joke on it, it sounds like a closing theme. Sort of like, 'Ladies and gentlemen, Miss Diana Ross!' and Diana walks off with the orchestra going. But if you see the joke, it comes after 'Lonely Old

People': nobody asked us to play, they're wondering what's going on, spending time, nobody gets involved with lonely old people. One of the big things for lonely old people in England is to watch *Crossroads*. That was it, just a joke at the end. Funnily enough, they're going to use it at the end of the [TV show] now, use our tune on it, which is great." Indeed, Wings' version was used to close the television programme and thus, for a short while, it became one of the most played tracks from the album.

### Venus And Mars data

The album was issued in a gatefold sleeve with cover photographs by Aubrey Powell (inner gatefold) and Linda (front cover). As the jacket did not feature the band's name, a circular sticker with 'WINGS' and red and yellow balls was adhered to the front cover. A printed inner sleeve, two posters, and two stickers completed the package.

The records were pressed with black and silver Capitol labels with red and yellow balls at 3 o'clock. American first pressings have 'manufactured by McCartney Music, Inc.' in the perimeter, while later editions have 'Manufactured by MPL Communications, Inc.' The LP was reissued by Columbia in 1980 (FC-36801 & JC-36801) and by EMI in 1988 on its Fame imprint (FA 3213).

The album was issued on 8-track in Britain (8X-PCTC 2541) and the USA (8XW 11525). In America, Capitol issued a quadraphonic mix on 8-track (Q8W 11419). When Columbia acquired the rights to McCartney's back catalogue, they reissued *Venus And Mars* on 8-track (JCA 36801).

*Venus And Mars* was issued on CD by Columbia on February 29 1984 (CK 36801). Capitol reissued the CD in November 1988 (CDP 7 46984 2) and DCC Compact Classics issued a gold CD (GZS-1067) in 1994. EMI issued the CD (CD-FA 3213) in Britain on October 19 1987 and issued a remastered edition (CDPMCOL6) on July 7 1993.

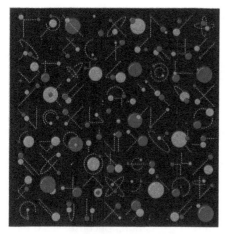

Venus And Mars inner sleeve

Above: stickers included with original copies of the album.

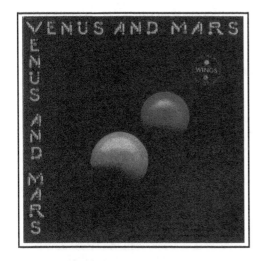

## 'LETTING GO' / 'YOU GAVE ME THE ANSWER'
## WINGS
**UK release** September 5 1975; Capitol R 6008; chart high No.41.
**US release** September 29 1975; Capitol 4145; chart high No.39.

### 'LETTING GO'
Alan Parsons, an accomplished engineer who worked on The Beatles' *Abbey Road* and
Pink Floyd's *Dark Side Of The Moon*, remixed 'Letting Go' at Abbey Road for release as
the second single from *Venus And Mars*. His remix shortened the introduction and
ending, placed the organ motif higher in the mix, and made McCartney's vocal much
drier. Despite this, it did not perform particularly well in the UK or US charts.

The single was issued with customised Capitol 'dome' labels in a plain sleeve.
Parlophone/Capitol issued demonstration copies of the single with 'DEMO RECORD
NOT FOR SALE' above the spindle hole and a large 'A' at 2 o'clock, with the release
date below. In the USA, Capitol issued mono/stereo edits of the A-side as a demonstration single, on PRO-8225.

**'VENUS AND MARS', 'ROCK SHOW' / 'MAGNETO AND TITANIUM MAN'**
**WINGS**
**UK release** November 28 1975; Capitol R 6010; failed to chart.
**US release** October 27 1975; Capitol 4175; chart high No.12.

'VENUS AND MARS'
The third and final single from *Venus And Mars* lifted three songs from Side 1 of the album. The A-side was an edit, which removed several seconds from 'Venus and Mars' and almost four minutes from 'Rock Show'. 'Magneto And Titanium Man' is the album version, complete.

Issued with customized Capitol 'dome' labels in a plain sleeve, 'Venus And Mars' failed to enter the British charts or stop the album's chart descent. It was, however, a hit in the USA.

Parlophone/Capitol issued demonstration copies of the single with 'DEMO RECORD NOT FOR SALE' above the spindle hole and a large 'A' at 2 o'clock, with the date 21.11.75 below. Capitol issued mono/stereo edits of the A-side as a demonstration single (PRO-8261).

# 1976: At The Speed Of Sound to Wings Over America

*AT THE SPEED OF SOUND*
WINGS
**Side 1** 'Let 'Em In', 'The Note You Never Wrote', 'She's My Baby', 'Beware My Love', 'Wino Junko'.
**Side 2** 'Silly Love Songs', 'Cook Of The House', 'Time To Hide', 'Must Do Something About It', 'San Ferry Anne', 'Warm And Beautiful'.
**UK release** March 26 1976; LP Parlophone PAS 10010; 8-track cartridge Parlophone 8X-PAS 10010; chart high No.2.
**US release** March 22 1976; LP Capitol SW-11525; 8-track cartridge Capitol 8XW-11525; chart high No.1.

### 'Let 'Em In' (McCartney)
Paul McCartney (bass, piano, vocals), Linda McCartney (keyboards, backing vocals), Denny Laine (guitar, backing vocals), Jimmy McCulloch (guitar), Joe English (drums), Steve 'Tex' Howard (trumpet), Thaddeus Richard (saxophone), Howie Casey (saxophone), Tony Dorsey (trombone).
### 'The Note You Never Wrote' (McCartney)
Paul McCartney (bass, backing vocals), Linda McCartney (keyboards, backing vocals), Denny Laine (guitar, vocals), Jimmy McCulloch (guitar), Joe English (drums).
### 'She's My Baby' (McCartney)
Paul McCartney (bass, vocals), Linda McCartney (keyboards, backing vocals), Denny Laine (guitar, backing vocals), Jimmy McCulloch (guitar), Joe English (drums).
### 'Beware My Love' (McCartney)
Personnel as 'She's My Baby'.
### 'Wino Junko' (McCulloch, Allen)
Paul McCartney (bass, backing vocals), Linda McCartney (keyboards, backing vocals), Denny Laine (guitar, backing vocals), Jimmy McCulloch (guitar, vocals), Joe English (drums).
### 'Silly Love Songs' (McCartney)
Personnel as 'Let 'Em In'.
### 'Cook Of The House' (McCartney)
Paul McCartney (upright bass, backing vocals), Linda McCartney (keyboards, vocals), Denny Laine (guitar, backing vocals), Jimmy McCulloch (guitar), Joe English (drums), Thaddeus Richard or Howie Casey (saxophone).
### 'Time To Hide' (Laine)
Paul McCartney (bass, backing vocals), Linda McCartney (keyboards, backing vocals), Denny Laine (guitar, vocals), Jimmy McCulloch (guitar), Joe English (drums), Steve 'Tex' Howard (trumpet), Thaddeus Richard (saxophone), Howie Casey (saxophone), Tony Dorsey (trombone).
### 'Must Do Something About It' (McCartney)
Paul McCartney (drums, backing vocals), Linda McCartney (keyboards, backing vocals), Denny Laine (bass, backing vocals), Jimmy McCulloch (guitar), Joe English (vocals).
### 'San Ferry Anne' (McCartney)
Personnel as 'Let 'Em In'.
### 'Warm And Beautiful' (McCartney)
Paul McCartney (piano, vocals), Denny Laine (guitar), Jimmy McCulloch (guitar).
All recorded at Abbey Road Studios, London, England. All produced by Paul McCartney.

## AT THE SPEED OF SOUND

Wings' Australian tour was to have been followed by dates in Japan. But McCartney was bared from entering the country at the last minute because of his convictions for possession of cannabis and so spent the time relaxing in Hawaii where he began planning his next album. Wings had done some recording in September, but on returning to Britain they booked into EMI Studios, Abbey Road, and worked on the album throughout January and February 1976.

Coming off the back of tour dates in Britain, Australia and Europe, Wings' fifth album was just that – a Wings album. Speaking at the time, McCartney claimed he wanted to move away from centre stage, because taking 'star' billing had become "an embarrassment". He said: "It was never Paul McCartney & The Beatles, Paul McCartney & The Quarrymen, or Paul McCartney & The Moondogs. Wings is quicker and easier to say, and everybody knows I'm in the group anyway." McCartney didn't really step out of the limelight, but he did allow other members of the band to bask in its glow, albeit briefly.

It seemed to do the trick. The Mk.5 line-up looked and sounded like a proper band rather than a bunch of sidemen. According to McCartney, Wings finally felt like a band. "As Denny says: 'It's a great group.' That old feeling," he said. But was it? Regardless of whose name appeared on the label, McCartney was the star, and like it or not the others would never threaten to dethrone their boss. Perhaps this line-up felt more like a band because McCartney finally had the right combination of musicians around him. It might have felt settled, but one year on and Wings would once again consist of the McCartney-Laine-McCartney core.

Wings apparent sense of togetherness did give them the confidence to take America by storm and rival The Beatles in terms of record and ticket sales. After several line-up changes and false starts, McCartney finally felt comfortable with the band he'd created and could relax, and that came across in the music Wings recorded for *At The Speed Of Sound*. Speaking to Chris Welch of the *Melody Maker*, McCartney said: "The album didn't take too long  it could have been done a lot quicker. We didn't rush it, but let the ideas blossom." The relaxed approach to recording did more than let the ideas blossom, it let the band blossom too.

McCartney gave everyone a vocal and let the horn section write their own parts, because "they can really get behind it, because it's their bit," he explained. While McCartney revised approach to managing the group could be seen as democracy, albeit on his terms, that didn't stop critics from attacking him for delegating vocal duties to less talented individuals. However, McCartney's gambit paid off, big time. Besides developing a stronger group identity, it resulted in Wings most commercial album since *Band On The Run*. An underrated gem of a record, *At The Speed Of Sound* is a near perfect pop album. McCartney's most successful US chart album, it is Wings' finest moment and contains at least one post-Beatles classic in 'Warm And Beautiful'.

### *At The Speed Of Sound* songs

The album opens with the sound of the McCartneys doorbell welcoming us to enter a relaxed, upbeat collection of songs. 'Let 'Em In' was originally written for Ringo Starr, but McCartney decided to keep it for himself and with good reason. It had hit written all over it. The song developed from a list of people he wanted to invite to a fantasy party. "That's what the song is about, it just sort of said there's someone knocking on the door, let 'em in. You know, let's have a party: why keep them outside? So in listing the kind of people who may be outside the door, I just naturally went to Auntie Gin, Brother Michael – Brother Michael being my own brother, Auntie Gin being my Auntie Gin – I mean, they all exist. Phil and Don being the Everly [Brothers]. I just wanted a parade of people that we could imagine outside the door, so I drew on the people I knew, really," he said.

Extending one of McCartney's favourite themes, domesticity, 'Let 'Em In' says little more than come in and chill out. It's a pure pop record that sounds great on the radio or at a party. With its heavy bass thump it appeared to pay lip service to the emergent disco scene which led some to speculate that it was axiomatic of McCartney's musical triviality. Not for the first time was he condemned for taking a populist approach – this was, after all, a pop record.

'The Note You Never Wrote' was the first song recorded for the album and given to Denny Laine to sing. McCartney recorded a guide vocal that was replaced by Laine's for the finished master. McCartney thought that thus far Laine's recordings with the band had been lightweight and he wanted him to record something more substantial. While Laine proffered a roughneck rocker of his own, 'Time To Hide', McCartney considered 'The Note You Never Wrote' epic enough to provide him with the kind of vehicle that best suited his talents.

Next comes 'She's My Baby', a song of love inspired by and dedicated to Linda. Like both singles taken from the album, it was indebted to the emergent vogue for bass-heavy dance records. Adopting the same formula he'd employed for 'Let 'Em In' and 'Silly Love Songs', McCartney placed the bottom end of Wings' rhythm section high in the mix. "That is the bass in your face. And that was really because we were making a dance record," he explained. A long time fan of R&B and soul, McCartney often fought to get more bass onto The Beatles' early records to make them 'dancer-friendly' and sound more American. A hybrid of genres, 'She's My Baby' reflects both the interests of its maker and the influence that American dance music was having on pop/rock music.

As if to dispel accusations that Wings were becoming a group of disco-loving softies, McCartney turned in 'Beware My Love', a mid-tempo rocker modelled on 'Soily' and 'Rock Show'. Replicating the band's live set-up in the studio, McCartney attempted to recreate the buzz of playing before an audience. "[We aimed to get all the] excitement in the backing track so it's human: you can hear we're all there," he explained. "Build on a great take and there's no problem. If it's a ropey take, which you're hoping to save further down the line – which I've also done – then it is a problem because it's like a rickety building that's going to fall down any minute. No foundations." 'Beware My Love' doesn't suffer from any such problems. Far from it, it's a rock solid beat number that sounded even better when Wings played it in-concert. A lengthy preamble, featuring Linda's multi-tracked vocals, precedes an especially expressive vocal from McCartney that evokes a feeling of emotional ambivalence, which his lyric suggests lies at the heart of any relationship.

Jimmy McCulloch co-wrote 'Wino Junko' with Stone The Crows drummer Colin Allen. Another song about alcohol and drug abuse, it is less weighty than McCulloch's contribution to *Venus And Mars*, but it nevertheless fits snugly alongside contributions from other members of the band. Its darker tone is masked by McCartney's airy production, which unfortunately tends to expose McCulloch's fragile vocal, a short-coming that could have been disguised with a few deft production touches.

The conflicting tone of McCulloch's lyric and melody led some to suggest that a process of musical assimilation was taking place within the band. Individuals were apparently tailoring their material to fit McCartney's style, rather than assert their own. This appeared to reveal the extent to which McCartney continued to dominate the group. Now Wings was a band it was only natural that its members would submit material that suited it rather than their solo ambitions. If they wanted to record outside of Wings they were free to just that.

McCulloch did just that. Forming White Line for solo excursions, he released a single, 'Too Many Miles', through EMI. If there were any musical differences within Wings at this time, the escape route of solo projects appeared to dissipate any dissent among the ranks or threats of a break-up. McCulloch certainly appeared contented. "Wings are settled for years. It would be a shame if anything happened," he said. "I can't see anything cracking Wings in the foreseeable future."

McCartney wrote 'Silly Love Songs' at the piano while on holiday in Hawaii. He then transposed the melody to the bass, purposely making it the lead instrument. "We really pushed the bass and drums right out front," he said. "But it pushed the song along quite nicely. Pushed it hard. We wanted to make something you could dance to."

McCartney is often considered a sentimentalist, and the cosy husband and wife interplay in 'Silly Love Songs' seemed to reinforce this view. However, McCartney said that the song was a considered response to these charges. "Originally, I wrote the song at about the time when the kind of material I did was a bit out of favour ... and you had Alice Cooper doing 'No More Mr Nice Guy' and that kind of hard parody. I rather picked up a feeling that ballads were being regarded as soppy and love songs as too sentimental."

For McCartney, 'Silly Love Songs' expressed sentiments that ran deeper than the song's seductive superficiality suggests. "You see, I'm looking at love not from the perspective of 'oh, boring old love,' I'm looking at it like when you get married and have a baby or something, that kind of love. I mean, that's pretty strong; it's not lurve, that stuff; it's something deeper."

McCartney's backhanded swipe at his critics was an attempt at ironic self-parody that many missed. The very title should have alerted the more astute to the fact that he was poking fun at his public image, as well as questioning those who criticised his values. McCartney wrote 'Silly Love Songs' in full knowledge of the criticism being levelled at him. As such, it's a knowing, ironic response to those who cast him as a sentimentalist and a self-referential celebration of his own values. (A reggae version was apparently attempted during the making of *At The Speed Of Sound*, but it remains unreleased. 'Silly Love Songs' would be re-recorded for *Give My Regards To Broad Street*, without improvement.)

In keeping with the spirit of *Speed Of Sound*, Linda was given a song written by her husband. 'Cook Of The House' is a 1950s-styled rocker, McCartney's tribute to his wife's culinary skills, written in November 1975 while Wings were touring Australia. "Late one night when we were on tour, renting a house in Australia, we were looking at one of those plaques found in many kitchens worldwide: 'Wherever I serve my guests, they like my kitchen best.' This led to a perusal of the contents of the shelves around us, which instantly became the lyric of the song," Paul said.

A light-hearted rock'n'roll track, 'Cook Of The House' reveals Paul and Linda's love of the genre. "I was a rock'n'roll kid," recalled Linda. "My first greatest moment was going to an Alan Freed Rhythm & Blues Show at the Brooklyn Paramount in about 1957, when I was a junior in high school." It features McCartney on Presley sideman Bill Black's double bass, and the recording was mixed to mono to make it sound that bit more authentic. Issued as the B-side of 'Silly Love Songs', it later surfaced on Linda's posthumous debut album, *Wide Prairie*.

Denny Laine's contribution, 'Time To Hide', was his first solo composition to feature on a Wings record since he joined the band in 1971. He released solo albums in 1973, 1976, and 1980, but has not been a prolific writer. Indeed, when performing live with Wings, he usually concentrated on material written or recorded in the 1960s, the one exception being 'Time To Hide'. As competent as anything McCartney contributed to the album, it became a staple of the Wings live set during their 1975/'76 world tour.

McCartney's allocation of songs to other members of the band didn't sit well with some critics who considered it a waste. One critic went as far as to suggest: "It's just about understandable letting your wife sing a track ... but to have drummer Joe English and [Denny] Laine have a go is simply not on when they're so obviously inferior singers to Paul himself." McCartney claimed otherwise. He gave 'Must Do Something About It' to Joe English because "there were a few [songs] I didn't really know what to do with. I put a backing down, then got the idea of getting Joe Engish to do it because he's got a very good voice."

Joe English's reading of 'Must Do Something About It', provided the biggest surprise on the album. He has a remarkably expressive voice, which McCartney enthused about: "He can sing well ... but [that performance is] nothing to what he could do." Far from being 'inferior', English's performance is on a par with anything on the album, and it's debatable whether anyone could have improved on it. When asked how he achieved it he joked "Well, I come from the New York ghetto". Actually, English wasn't joking. Interviewed for *Wings Fun Club* magazine he explained: "I went through the stage of playing Wilson Pickett and James Brown  all white bands playing that while I was practically living in a ghetto with nearly all Blacks and Puerto Ricans. Of course it did have an influence on me, which is why I'm going through an adjustment period playing the music I'm playing now."

'Must Do Something About It' was the ideal vehicle for his vocal mannerisms, which perfectly matched the blue-eyed-soul feel that McCartney was aiming for. With English given the lead vocal, McCartney jumped on drums for this song and delivered a solid performance that would have fooled many into believing that it was Wings regular drummer on the track rather than its bassist. Segued with Laine's 'Time To Hide', the song has a summery disposition and rolling cadence that offsets what in other hands could have become a morose lyric about loneliness.

'San Ferry Anne' is the antithesis of 'Must Do Something About It', as self-confident as the latter is self-effacing. This is pop, pure and simple, it demands little and, like the lifestyle to which it alludes, is a glamorous affirmation of the high-life.

If one song can be said to capture McCartney at his most idealistic, it's *Speed Of Sound*'s closing track, 'Warm And Beautiful'. A simple eight-bar phrase introduces the central motif, which, depending on one's point of view, is either compelling or tedious. McCartney's piano accompaniment supports a delicate interpretation of a lyric steeped in romantic idealism, which in the hands of others could have degenerated into mawkish pap. But his epistle to Linda is rescued by a typically mobile melody. Although the lyric is perhaps too idealised, the song's sweeping melody and McCartney's warm delivery largely dispose of any suggestions of mawkishness. A favourite of McCartney's, 'Warm And Beautiful' was at one point considered fit for release as a single but was overlooked in favour of more up-tempo material.

'Warm And Beautiful' 7-inch acetate cut at PRT Studios.

### At The Speed Of Sound data

Despite mixed reviews and the fact that Wings were competing with a renewed interest in The Beatles – EMI reissued all of The Beatles' singles, almost all of which found their way back into the charts – *At The Speed Of Sound* fared remarkably well, spending 30 weeks in the British charts to become the forth bestselling British album of 1976 and 51 weeks on the US charts, including seven (non-consecutive) weeks at Number 1.

The album was issued with customised 'Speed Of Sound' labels and printed inner sleeve. Linda took the cover photograph and Humphrey Ocean drew the picture for the inner sleeve, which depicts members of Kilburn & The Highroads (Ocean had played bass guitar in that band and was taught at art college by their singer, Ian Dury). Because the cover did not make it clear that this was Wings' new LP, Capitol manufactured a circular sticker with 'WINGS' in white text on a black background over a large 'W', which was adhered to the front cover. Columbia reissued the LP (FC-37409 & PC 37409) with generic red labels on 13 July 1981.

The album was issued on 8-track in Britain (8X-PAS 10010) and the USA (8XW 11525). It was reissued by Columbia (JCA 37409) in the early 1980s.

EMI issued *At The Speed Of Sound* on CD (CDP7481992) on July 10 1989 and issued a remastered edition (CDPMCOL7) on July 7 1993. Capitol issued the CD (CDP 7 48199 2) on June 20 1989.

## 'SILLY LOVE SONGS' / 'COOK OF THE HOUSE'
WINGS
**UK release** April 30 1976; Parlophone R 6014; chart high No.2.
**US release** April 1 1976; Capitol 4256; chart high No.1.

### 'SILLY LOVE SONGS'
Released in America at the height of Wingsmania, 'Silly Love Songs' became Wings' forth single to top the American charts. In the UK it stalled at number 2, kept from the top spot by 'Combine Harvester', a novelty hit by British west-country group The Wurzels.

In recent years, 'Silly Love Songs' has been remixed, sampled, and reissued on several promotional records. To promote *Wingspan – Hits And History*, McCartney commissioned three remixes, which were issued in Germany as a promotional CD (CDP 000587). These remixes were also issued in Italy by the Dance Factory label as a 12-inch single (7243 880073 6 8). In Britain, a 'Wings vs Loop Da Loop Mix' was issued as a promotional 12-inch single (12-WINDJ-002) backed with 'Coming Up' in a 'Linus Loves Mix'. According to the press release, only 50 copies of this record were pressed. In Holland, Lifted Records issued a house mix by Noir and Krusé as a CD single (334 50881). A sample from 'Silly Love Songs', licensed by MPL, was used for Jenn Cuneta's 'Come Rain Come Shine', a Top 5 single on the *Billboard* dance chart in 2005.

For its original release, Parlophone and Capitol issued 'Silly Love Songs' with customised *'Speed Of Sound'* labels in a plain paper sleeve. In America, the single was also issued with black and silver Capitol 'dome' labels and later purple and silver 'dome' labels.

Parlophone issued a demonstration 7-inch single with edited (A-side) and full length versions (B-side). The label has a large white 'A' above the spindle hole and (EDITED VERSION) below the song title. In the USA, Capitol issued a demonstration 7-inch single (P-4256) with white labels with black text and the Capitol logo top centre and 'NOT FOR SALE' bottom centre below 'WINGS'. The single featured edited and full-length versions of the A-side. Columbia reissued the single (18-02171) in 1981 with generic orange and yellow labels.

**'LET 'EM IN' / 'BEWARE MY LOVE'**
**WINGS**
**UK release** July 23 1976; Parlophone R 6015; chart high No.2.
**US release** June 28 1976; Capitol 4293; chart high No.3.

'LET 'EM IN'
With *At The Speed Of Sound* beginning its chart descent, a second hit from the album was required to boost album sales. Doubly successful, 'Let 'Em In' reached the Top 5 in both Britain and the USA and pushed the album back into the Top 10. 'Let 'Em In' got an extra lease of chart life when Billy Paul hit with the song in the early months of 1977. Twenty-five years later, the song was remixed to promote *Wingspan – Hits And History*, and it was sampled and used to underpin 'Inside Thing', a duet between McCartney and Lulu that appeared on her 2002 album, *Together*.

As with the previous single, 'Let 'Em In' was issued with customised *'Speed Of Sound'* labels in a plain paper sleeve. In America, the single was also manufactured by Capitol with black and silver 'dome' labels.

In Britain, Parlophone issued a demonstration 7-inch single with a stereo edit on the A-side and the full-length version on the B-side. The label has a large white 'A' above the spindle hole, 'DEMO RECORD NOT FOR SALE' on three lines below the spindle hole, and (EDITED VERSION) below the song title.

Capitol issued a 7-inch demonstration single (P-4293) with white labels with black text and the Capitol logo top centre and 'NOT FOR SALE' bottom centre, below 'WINGS'. The single featured a mono edit and the full-length stereo version of the A-side.

In France, the single was issued in a fake leopard-skin sleeve as a 12-inch single (2C 052 98062 Y), the first time one of McCartney's records had been released commercially on this format. Another European oddity was the release of 'Let 'Em In' on the Apple label in Turkey (2C 006-98062). Although Apple was officially no more, nobody had bothered to tell the Turks, who issued the single on the Apple label with a picture sleeve six months after the company had ceased to issue records by the ex-Fabs.

## WE MOVED!
'Let 'Em In' / 'Silly Love Songs' / 'My Love' / 'Live And Let Die' / 'Tragedy'
'Jet' / 'Band On The Run' / 'Uncle Albert'
WINGS / PAUL & LINDA McCARTNEY
**UK release** September 1976

### 'Tragedy' (Wayne)
Paul McCartney (vocals, bass), Linda McCartney (backing vocals), Denny Laine
(guitar, backing vocals), Henry McCullough (guitar, guitar-sitar), Denny Seiwell
(drums). Recorded at AIR Studios or Abbey Road Studios, London, England.

Issued to promote MPL's growing music publishing business, and to alert music
business insiders to the fact that it had just moved to 1 Soho Square, London, *We
Moved!* featured clips of songs published by the company. Alongside songs by Frank
Sinatra, Buddy Holly and Judy Garland were several by Wings. Among them was the
unreleased 'Tragedy'. Written by Thomas Wayne and originally issued by Sun Records,
Wings recorded the song during sessions for *Red Rose Speedway*. McCartney intend-
ing to release it on the *Cold Cuts* album which, despite continued work, was itself
scrapped. A cute ballad that McCartney sings as if he'd written it himself, it is indeed
a tragedy that this song remains locked away in McCartney's archives. However, it has
been widely bootlegged.

what's happened
to us? . . . . .

1 Soho Square Photographed from Centrepoint.

. . . . . we moved!

## TO 1 SOHO SQUARE

MPL (McCartney Productions Limited)
home of Wings, McCartney Music,
E. H. Morris, The Buddy Holly Catalogue,
The Jack Lawrence Catalogue,
Morley Music, MPL Book Publishing, MPL Films,
has moved from 12–13 Greek Street, London W1
to new premises at
**1 Soho Square, London W1V 6BQ.**
**Telephone: 01-439 6621**
**Telex: 21294.**

Drawing based on 1 Soho Square from MPL animated film "Oriental Night Fish" by Ian Emes.

*WINGS OVER AMERICA*

WINGS

**Side 1** 'Venus And Mars', 'Rock Show', 'Jet', 'Let Me Roll It', 'Spirits Of Ancient Egypt', 'Medicine Jar'.

**Side 2** 'Maybe I'm Amazed', 'Call Me Back Again', 'Lady Madonna', 'The Long And Winding Road', 'Live And Let Die'.

**Side 3**: 'Picasso's Last Words', 'Richard Cory', 'Bluebird', 'I've Just Seen A Face', 'Blackbird', 'Yesterday'.

**Side 4**: 'You Gave Me The Answer', 'Magneto And Titanium Man', 'Go Now', 'My Love', 'Listen To What The Man Said'.

**Side 5**: 'Let 'Em In', 'Time To Hide', 'Silly Love Songs', 'Beware My Love'.

**Side 6**: 'Letting Go', 'Band On The Run', 'Hi, Hi, Hi', 'Soily'.

**UK release** December 10 1976; LP Parlophone PCSP 720; 8-track cartridge Parlophone 8X-PCSP 720; chart high No.8.

**US release** December 10 1976; LP Capitol SWCO-11593; 8-track cartridge Capitol 8X3C-11593; chart high No.1.

### 'Lady Madonna' (Lennon, McCartney)

Paul McCartney (piano, vocals), Linda McCartney (keyboards, backing vocals), Denny Laine (bass), Jimmy McCulloch (guitar), Joe English (drums), Steve 'Tex' Howard (trumpet), Thaddeus Richard (saxophone), Howie Casey (saxophone), Tony Dorsey (trombone). Live recording at Olympia Stadium, Detroit, MI, USA.

### 'The Long And Winding Road' (Lennon, McCartney)

Personnel as 'Lady Madonna'. Live recording at Kemper Arena, Kansas City, KS, USA.

### 'Richard Cory' (Simon)

Paul McCartney (guitar), Denny Laine (guitar, vocals), Jimmy McCulloch (guitar). Live recording at The Forum, Los Angeles, CA, USA.

### 'I've Just Seen A Face' (Lennon, McCartney)

Paul McCartney (guitar, vocals), Linda McCartney (backing vocals), Denny Laine (guitar), Jimmy McCulloch (bass), Joe English (drums). Live recording at The Forum, Los Angeles, CA, USA.

### 'Blackbird' (Lennon, McCartney)

Paul McCartney (guitar, vocals). Live recording at Boston Garden, Boston, MA, USA.

### 'Yesterday' (Lennon, McCartney)

Paul McCartney (guitar, vocals), Steve 'Tex' Howard (trumpet), Thaddeus Richard (saxophone), Howie Casey (saxophone), Tony Dorsey (trombone). Recording location unknown. Produced by Paul McCartney.

### 'Go Now' (Banks, Bennett)

Paul McCartney (bass), Linda McCartney (keyboards, backing vocals), Denny Laine (piano, vocals), Jimmy McCulloch (guitar), Joe English (drums), Steve 'Tex' Howard (trumpet), Thaddeus Richard (saxophone), Howie Casey (saxophone), Tony Dorsey (trombone). Live recording at The Forum, Los Angeles, CA, USA.

### 'Soily' (McCartney)

Paul McCartney (bass, vocals), Linda McCartney (keyboards, backing vocals), Denny Laine (guitar), Jimmy McCulloch (guitar), Joe English (drums), Steve 'Tex' Howard (trumpet), Thaddeus Richard (saxophone), Howie Casey (saxophone), Tony Dorsey (trombone). Live recording at McNichols Sports Arena, Denver, CO, USA.

All produced by Paul McCartney.

WINGS OVER AMERICA

While John Lennon was preparing to take a break from the limelight, his former songwriting partner was readying himself for an extended period in its full glare. McCartney had been building up to a world tour with Wings for years. Beginning with a short tour of English universities, followed six months later by a European tour, McCartney had spent hours rehearsing and even longer developing his repertoire before taking it to the world and cementing his reputation as a seriously good solo artist.

Rehearsals were held at Elstree Studios, Borehamwood, north-west of London, where Wings gave a full dress performance to a specially invited audience of fans and record-company employees on September 6 1975. The tour opened three days later at the Southampton Gaumont before moving on to Australia, Europe, and North America. Speaking to *Melody Maker* about his plans for the tour, McCartney said: "In England ... the normal venues are like 3,000 [capacity], so very naturally we started off with 3,000 people, and then we went to 5,000, 6,000, 14,000 in Australia, and then we played some bigger halls in Europe, which were more like 15,000. ... I like things like that. I like things step by step."

By the time Wings hit America, both band and tour machine were performing to perfection, and McCartney's confidence was justified. "We've spent months rehearsing Wings. And it's all been better than I thought it would be," he rejoiced. Linda shared his enthusiasm in the band, which she believed came across in its performances. "Paul didn't feel confidence in the band before," she said, "whereas this band, he really knows he can get up there and sing."

But not everything went to plan. Jimmy McCulloch fell and damaged his hand after the band's Paris gig on March 26 1976, delaying the American leg of the tour by a month. The tour eventually opened at Fort Worth, Texas, on May 3. Speaking after the show McCartney admitted to being nervous, but his anxiety had been unfounded because Wings went down a storm. "I used to get much more nervous with The Beatles," he said. "I love American audiences. They're just great. The response to 'Live And Let Die' it was ridiculous."

Reviewing the Fort Worth gig for the *New York Times*, John Rockwell said: "This performance, however, sounded tougher and more overtly rock'n'roll than the recorded version. The arrangements were often very similar, but the whole tone was harder-edged, and McCartney's music benefited from the difference." Wings shows were, for the most part, received favourably, but not everybody was impressed. Reviewing Wings Los Angeles show, Lee Margules suggested that: "The main problem, however, was that Wings had little to offer. Although the musicianship on the 30 songs performed during the two hour 15 minute concert was technically sound, it lacked the individual distinction or inspiration to make it exciting." Wings wasn't about individual showmanship or virtuosity, McCartney's musical vision had to be strictly adhered to. Although he'd given members of Wings space to express themselves within the band, Wings was his band, this was his tour and he was the star.

Most, if not all, of Wings American shows were recorded, and on his return to Britain McCartney began listening to the best of the recordings. "Our sound engineer has listened to 800 hours of tape (from the American tour) and selected the top five takes of each tune," McCartney explained. "we're now going through those five takes, that's five takes of 30 tunes. We'll re-mix them and made a three-record set." The task was considerable and took six weeks to complete with McCartney reportedly working up to 14 hours a day to get the album ready in time for a Christmas release.

*Wings Over America* represents a complete live show, capturing the band at its most dynamic and powerful. Wings' set drew on some of the strongest material from McCartney's back catalogue, with songs drawn from Wings' three most recent albums: five songs from *Band On The Run*, five from *Venus And Mars*, and four from *Speed Of Sound*. And for the first time, McCartney included songs recorded by The Beatles, something he'd previously avoided. George Harrison performed several Beatles songs during his 1974 American tour. But while Harrison re-arranged the songs, and in certain cases re-wrote the lyrics, McCartney stuck to the original templates. McCartney finally had to acknowledge that a sizable chunk of his audience wanted the hear him sing Beatles songs. "The older people in the audience want to hear some of those songs, and for them we put them in," he admitted. "Originally I thought, 'Oh blimey, we can't do those old numbers'. But if nobody else does those songs they just become legends and die. We play them so people can come hear us do them."

Such a large tour inevitably created a number of associated projects. As well as recording many of Wings concerts for release on record, the tour was filmed with a cinema release in mind. The resulting film, *Rock Show*, eventually premiered in New York City on November 26 1980 and received a limited cinema release before making it to video. To promote the movie, Miramax Films produced a one-sided 7-inch single (CPS-4202) that featured three 'radio spots'. (The single was manufactured with a white label with black text.) In addition to the film, other mediums were used to make a visual record of the tour. Humphrey Ocean, who had drawn the inner sleeve for *Speed Of Sound*, became artist in residence for the American leg of the tour. Commissioned to make paintings and drawings inspired by his travels with the band, Ocean eventually published his work as *Ocean Way*. A photo documentary, *Hands Across The Water – Wings Tour USA* was produced as a book by Hipgnosis.

### Wings Over America songs
As with the rest of this book, live recordings already covered in their studio versions are not included in concert-record entries. So, for our purposes, the first 'new' track on *Wings Over America* is 'Lady Madonna'. Borrowing the piano lick from 'Bad Penny Blues', a 1956 hit for Humphrey Lyttelton, McCartney wrote it in celebration of motherhood. In concert, Wings take the song at a slightly faster tempo than The Beatles' studio recording. Nevertheless, it's a faithful reading and comes complete with an accurate transcription of the original improvised saxophone arrangement.

'The Long And Winding Road' was released by The Beatles on their swansong album, *Let It Be*, but McCartney all but disowned the original version because of Phil Spector's heavy-handed production. Although he may have abhorred Spector's production, the legendary producer had no choice other than to swamp the song with his 'wall of sound', as The Beatles' recording was little more than a rough sketch. The Beatles never returned to the song as by the time they completed the follow-up recording, *Abbey Road*, no one could face the job. Wings' reading has the advantage of a new synoptic introduction and fanfare-like horn arrangement, but Denny Laine's bass playing, albeit an improvement on Lennon's attempts, is still far too plodding.

'Richard Cory', sung by Laine, was written by Paul Simon and originally recorded by Simon & Garfunkel for their album *Sound Of Silence*. Performed during Wings' acoustic set, a forerunner of the unplugged format, the song was programmed as a medley with 'Picasso's Last Words', also sung mainly by Laine. A piece of social commentary that no doubt went down well with student audiences in the mid 1960s, 'Richard Cory' is the tale of a capitalist who comes to a sticky end.

'I've Just Seen A Face' is another Beatles song, this time from *Help!*, and was originally an instrumental, 'Auntie Gin's Theme', until McCartney added the lyric. He would return to the song 25 years later when he performed it with Paul Simon at the Adopt-A-Minefield gala held at the Beverly Wilshire Hotel in Los Angeles.

Recorded for The Beatles' *White Album*, the acoustic ballad 'Blackbird' apparently came to McCartney with words and music complete. Inspired by a piece by Bach that he and George Harrison used to impress people with at parties, 'Blackbird' was a metaphor for Afro-American emancipation. As McCartney explained to Terry Gross: "'Blackbird' was something I wrote in the 1960s, and I used to play a kind of version of a Bach piece. I used to play a ... fingerpicking thing on that. [The] music was inspired by that. And then the words were actually to do with the civil rights movement. I was imagining a Blackbird being symbolic for a young black woman living in America at the time, experiencing the injustices that were going on then, particularly. And this was hopefully to be an inspirational song where ... even though she was going through all these terrible times, she'll be able to look and listen to this song and be inspired by it to continue to fight against the injustices."

Evidence that this is indeed what he intended and not historical revisionism can be found on a tape McCartney recorded with Donovan and Mary Hopkin while working on Hopkin's *Postcard* album. Having performed 'Blackbird', he jokes about playing the song to Diana Ross, who took offence (at being called a black bird). He then explains that "I'd read somewhere in the papers about riots and that". Whatever the inspiration, the clever use of slang combined with powerful imagery and a typically mobile McCartney melody created an enduring song of hope and aspiration.

McCartney claims he awoke one morning with the music for 'Yesterday' running through his head. At first he thought he must have heard the song elsewhere and played it to friends asking if they had ever heard it. He continued to work on the song throughout 1964, rewriting the lyrics and perfecting the melody, until confident enough to commit the song to tape. The Beatles were unable to come up with an arrangement, and Lennon suggested that McCartney should record the song with just acoustic guitar. Thus armed, McCartney taped the song at Abbey Road on the evening of 14 June 1965. Only two takes were recorded, the second being marked best (the first was later released on *Anthology 2*). At George Martin's suggestion, a string quartet was overdubbed three days later, but not without reservations from McCartney, who saw The Beatles as a rock band and thought strings unsuited to the band's image. Nevertheless, Martin persevered and persuaded him that a small string section would enhance the song. Newly convinced, McCartney helped write the arrangement with the proviso that the players used no vibrato, lest they end up sounding like the records of easy-listening king Mantovani.

The resulting song was a Number 1 single in America, but in Britain it remained buried on Side 2 of *Help!*, where there was less chance of it tarnishing the band's image. It was issued on an EP in Britain, but by then the format was beginning to loose popularity and the 'Yesterday' EP failed to make the British charts. The song was eventually released as a single in Britain in 1976, when The Beatles' singles catalogue, along with two new couplings, 'Yesterday' / 'I Should Have Known Better' (R 6013) and 'Back In The USSR' / 'Twist And Shout' (R 6016), were issued by EMI. Despite its popularity, the song failed to make Number 1 in Britain, only managing Number 8. When released in 1965, it became something of an instant classic – in other words, it became a success for others. It eventually became one of the most covered songs in recording history, with some 2,000 versions to its credit, and went on to become the most played song on American radio with a total of seven million plays.

Bessie Banks recorded 'Go Now' in 1963, but The Moody Blues, with Denny Laine on vocals, had the hit the following year. Wings here reproduce the Moody Blues treatment, which they augment with a new horn arrangement and a restrained solo from Jimmy McCulloch. Whilst comparable to the Moody Blues reading, Wings' interpretation adds little to the original and was undoubtedly included to give Laine another vocal during the band's concerts.

The only new McCartney song to grace the album had been kicking around for a few years. Wings performed 'Soily' regularly during tours of Europe and Britain in 1972/'73. Originally shorter, slower, and less dynamic than the version on *Wings Over America*, it was intended for the *Red Rose Speedway* album, initially planned as a double LP, but dropped at the last moment. Now with the hottest Wings line-up behind it, 'Soily' had acquired a quasi-heavy metal arrangement and, thanks to some energetic drumming from Joe English, a tough dynamic. The addition of a horn arrangement helped transform 'Soily' into a piece of explosive rock hyperbole perfect for stadium performances and an ideal song with which to end *Wings Over America*.

### Wings Over America data
*Wings Over America* was issued as a three-record set, with each LP having unique customised labels, and printed inner sleeves. Designed by the McCartneys and Hipgnosis, the package, which included a poster, was housed in a gatefold sleeve. Richard Manning provided the front cover painting, which symbolised Wings' arrival in America. A door in the side of an aircraft opens, revealing a shaft of bright white light which represents either a curtain being drawn back or music streaming from a stage. The theme is continued on the inner sleeves, the aperture becoming larger as it spreads across the three inner covers.

Miramax Films radio promo

The album was issued on 8-track in Britain (8X-PCSP 720) and the USA (8X3C-11593). It was Wings' last album to be issued on 8-track in Britain. EMI issued the album as a two-CD set (CDP7481992) on May 25 1987; Columbia issued the CD (CK-37990/1) on February 29 1984; and Capitol reissued the CD (CDP 7 46715/6 2) on January 17 1988.

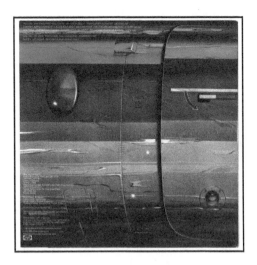

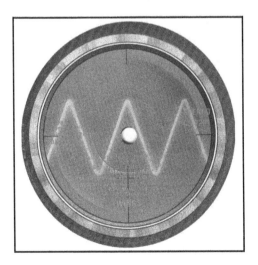

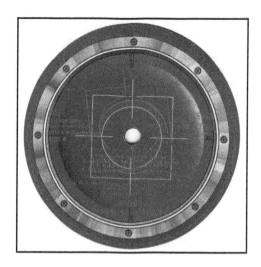

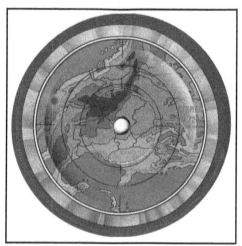

Sticker attached to original copies
of the album.

1977: Maybe I'm Amazed to Mull of Kintyre

## 'MAYBE I'M AMAZED' / 'SOILY'
## WINGS
**UK release** February 4 1977; Parlophone R 6017; chart high No.28.
**US release** February 7 1977; Capitol 4385; chart high No.10.

'MAYBE I'M AMAZED'

What should have made a stunning debut solo single for McCartney was instead relegated years later to this, little more than a tool to promote *Wings Over America*. 'Maybe I'm Amazed' managed only two weeks in the UK Top 30 but was a Top 10 hit in the USA.

Parlophone and Capitol issued the single with customised labels in a plain paper sleeve. (In Canada, Capitol issued a blue vinyl version of the single.) Parlophone issued a 7-inch demonstration single with a large grey 'A' above the spindle hole and 'DEMO RECORD NOT FOR SALE' on three lines below the spindle hole.

In America, Capitol issued a 7-inch demonstration single (PRO-8570) that featured mono/stereo versions of the A-side with black and sliver 'dome' labels. Capitol also issued a promotional 12-inch single ((S)PRO-8574) with mono/stereo edits of the A-side. A mono edit and album version were issued on side one, a stereo edit and album version on side two. The 12-inch record was issued in a black sleeve with Wings' logo centre top and 'Maybe I'm Amazed from the album "Wings over America"' below. Capitol Records' logo appears bottom centre and 'NOT FOR SALE' in the bottom right corner of the sleeve.

**'UNCLE ALBERT/ADMIRAL HALSEY' / 'EAT AT HOME'**
**PERCY 'THRILLS' THRILLINGTON**
**UK release** April 1977; Regal Zonophone EMI 2594; failed to chart.

**'Uncle Albert/Admiral Halsey' (Paul and Linda McCartney)**
Vic Flick (guitar), Clem Cattini (drums), Herbie Flowers (bass, tuba solo), Steve Gray (piano), Jim Lawless (percussion), The Mike Sammes Singers (vocals), unknown (strings), unknown (brass, woodwind).
**'Eat At Home' (Paul and Linda McCartney)**
Clem Cattini (drums), Herbie Flowers (bass), Roger Coulan (organ), Jim Lawless (percussion), The Mike Sammes Singers (vocals), unknown (brass, woodwind).
Both recorded at Abbey Road Studios, London, England. Both produced by Paul McCartney.

**'UNCLE ALBERT'**
Who is Percy Thrillington? That was a question asked by many in early 1977. His name had appeared in several London newspapers, resulting in a small avalanche of media speculation that helped fuel interest in this unknown recording artist. The answer was, of course, Paul McCartney. Issued by Regal Zonophone with generic red and silver labels, 'Uncle Albert/Admiral Halsey' / 'Eat At Home' failed to inspire many to rush out and buy the record or the album that followed.

Regal Zonophone issued a 7-inch demonstration single with a large 'A' at 2 o'clock and 'DEMO RECORD NOT FOR SALE' on three lines above the spindle hole.

*RAM*
## PERCY 'THRILLS' THRILLINGTON
**Side 1** 'Too Many People', '3 Legs', 'Ram On', 'Dear Boy', 'Uncle Albert/Admiral Halsey', 'Smile Away'.
**Side 2** 'Heart Of The Country', 'Monkberry Moon Delight', 'Eat At Home', 'Long Haired Lady', 'The Back Seat Of My Car'.
**UK release** April 29 1977; Regal Zonophone EMC 3175; failed to chart.
**US release** May 16 1977; LP Capitol ST-11642; 8-track cartridge Capitol 8XT-11642; failed to chart.

**'Too Many People'** (McCartney)
Clem Cattini (drums), Herbie Flowers (bass), Jim Lawless (percussion), The Mike Sammes Singers (vocals), unknown (brass).
**'3 Legs'** (McCartney)
Vic Flick (guitar), Clem Cattini (drums), Herbie Flowers (bass), Jim Lawless (percussion), unknown (brass).
**'Ram On'** (McCartney)
Vic Flick (guitar), Clem Cattini (drums), Herbie Flowers (bass), Jim Lawless (percussion), The Mike Sammes Singers (vocals), unknown (brass, woodwind), unknown (harp).
**'Dear Boy'** (Paul and Linda McCartney)
Clem Cattini (drums), Herbie Flowers (bass), Jim Lawless (percussion), The Mike Sammes Singers (vocals).
**'Uncle Albert/Admiral Halsey'** (Paul and Linda McCartney)
Vic Flick (guitar), Clem Cattini (drums), Herbie Flowers (bass, tuba solo), Steve Gray (piano), Jim Lawless (percussion), The Mike Sammes Singers (vocals), unknown (strings), unknown (brass, woodwind).
**'Smile Away'** (McCartney)
Vic Flick (guitar), Clem Cattini (drums), Herbie Flowers (bass), Jim Lawless (percussion), Chris Karen (cuica drum), unknown (brass).
**'Heart Of The Country'** (Paul and Linda McCartney)
Vic Flick (guitar), Clem Cattini (drums), Herbie Flowers (bass), Jim Lawless (percussion), The Mike Sammes Singers (vocals), unknown (woodwind).
**'Monkberry Moon Delight'** (Paul and Linda McCartney)
Clem Cattini (drums), Herbie Flowers (bass), Jim Lawless (percussion), unknown (brass), unknown (strings).
**'Eat At Home'** (Paul and Linda McCartney)
Clem Cattini (drums), Herbie Flowers (bass), Roger Coulan (organ), Jim Lawless (percussion), The Mike Sammes Singers (vocals), unknown (brass, woodwind).
**'Long Haired Lady'** (McCartney)
Vic Flick (guitar), Clem Cattini (drums), Herbie Flowers (bass), Jim Lawless (percussion), The Mike Sammes Singers (vocals), unknown (brass, woodwind).
**'The Back Seat Of My Car'** (McCartney)
Vic Flick (guitar), Clem Cattini (drums), Herbie Flowers (bass), Steve Gray (piano), Jim Lawless (percussion), Carl Dolmetsch Family (recorders), unknown (strings), unknown (brass). All recorded at Abbey Road Studios, London, England. All produced by Paul McCartney. Recording Studio: Abbey Road Studios, London. Producer: Paul McCartney.

## RAM/THRILLINGTON

Percy Thrillington was the first act signed to McCartney's MPL company. However, Mr Thrillington was a completely fictitious individual, as was the enigmatic Clint Harrigan who wrote the sleevenotes for this and Wings' debut album. Thrillington and Harrigan were pseudonyms used by McCartney, who went to considerable lengths to convince the public that they existed. Not only were business cards produced for Percy Thrillington, Paul and Linda even wrote his biography and took his photograph. "So we invented it all," admitted McCartney, "Linda and I, and we went around southern Ireland and found a guy in a field, a young farmer, and asked if he minded doing some photographic modelling for us. We wanted to find someone that no one could possibly trace, paid him the going rate, and photographed him in a field, wearing a sweater and then wearing an evening suit. But he never quite looked Percy Thrillington enough."

The *Thrillington* album was recorded over three days (June 15–17) in 1971 and resulted, among other things, from McCartney's desire to do something different with the songs he'd recorded for *Ram*. Explaining why he made the album, he said: "It all came about because I wanted someone to do a big-band version of *Ram* – but there were no takers, [so] I thought that I'd better be that someone."

McCartney's interest in the big-band era dates back to his childhood, when the sounds of bandleaders such as Glenn Miller and Ted Heath were practically all that was played on the conservative BBC. His fascination spread to writing convincing pastiches of old-time standards of the 1930s ('Honey Pie', 'You Gave Me The Answer') and employing big-band arrangements in songs such as 'You Want Her Too'.

To help him realise the project, McCartney called on the talents of Richard Hewson, who had orchestrated 'Those Were The Days', a song McCartney produced for the Apple recording artist Mary Hopkin. McCartney gave Hewson the freedom to orchestrate the songs however he wanted; McCartney's only stipulation was that he record with a relatively small 'pops' orchestra. Hewson was allowed to select the session musicians he wanted. "The musicians I chose were the small group of top players that I regularly used," he told Ian Peel. "Herbie Flowers on bass, Clem Cattini of The Tornados on drums, Vic Flick, a legendary guitarist, Roger Coulan on keyboards, the Dolmetsch family on recorders, The Mike Sammes Singers, and various top jazz players on saxes and brass, because I was and still am heavily into jazz. The strings and woodwind were all drawn from top session players of the day."

Although it was recorded in 1971, the *Thrillington* album was not issued until 1977. Released at the height of punk rock, its easy-listening style placed it at odds with contemporary musical trends. It was, however, as radical as any punk record; perhaps more so. Rather than play the punk card – McCartney did consider releasing a punk song, 'Boil Crisis' – he issued an easy-listening version of an album that was the best part of six years old. *Thrillington* was a bold experiment that presented some of his most complex and melodic compositions in a new light. It may even have been a clever ironic statement that poked fun at critics who claimed that, post-Beatles, all he could produce was muzak.

To promote both single and album, MPL placed a number of cryptic advertisements in the personal columns of *The Evening Standard* and *The Times* newspapers. This low-cost, inventive advertising campaign eventually led to an article in the *Evening Standard* that attempted to uncover the identity of the elusive Thrillington. As McCartney explained: "Then we started this whole business in *The Evening Standard* ad columns, which was the really fun thing, putting in things like 'Must get in touch with … Thrillington', as a result of which the newspaper columns picked up on it – 'Has anyone seen this rubbish going on in *The Evening Standard* about Percy Thrillington?' – and it was good publicity. It was one of our madcap publicity schemes, as if we were managing this character called Percy Thrillington."

For McCartney, at least, it did not really matter who controlled this project, as the whole Thrillington idea took on a conceptual feel. "You could say that Percy Thrillington was Richard Hewson, or just a fictitious leader of a band who never appeared anywhere," he explained. Conceptual joke or not, Thrillington is one of the more intriguing of McCartney's albums.

EMI helped promote the album with an elaborate advertising campaign that included 5-inch-diameter 'thought bubble' stickers, publicity photographs, Percy Thrillington business cards and radio 'tease' advertisements.

### Ram/Thrillington data

The album was issued in Britain by Regal Zonophone with generic red and silver labels. The cover painting, by Jeff Cummings, depicted a violinist with a ram's head. Cummings continued this theme on the rear cover and included McCartney's face, reflected in the window dividing the control room from the studio floor – a clue, if ever there was one, to McCartney's involvement. A thick black card inner sleeve completed the package. In the USA, Capitol issued the album with purple Capitol labels. Capitol also issued the album on 8-track (8XT 11642).

*Thrillington* was released on CD on May 1 1995, which was a considerable achievement in itself. As McCartney noted: "What I didn't realise was that no one would want to release an album like that. Not even then. And no way would it get released now." The CD release received next to no publicity, few shops bothered to stock it, and it was deleted relatively quickly. Consequently, fans missed the opportunity to purchase a copy and it became a rarity itself. However, the CD was reissued on June 7 2004 with identical packaging and label artwork to the original, the only difference being 'MADE IN EU' at bottom centre of the CD label, replacing 'MADE IN THE UNITED KINGDOM'.

**'SEASIDE WOMAN' / 'B SIDE TO SEASIDE'**
SUZY AND THE RED STRIPES
**UK release** August 10 1979; A&M AMS 7461; 7-inch boxed set A&M AMSP 7461; failed to chart.
**US release** May 31 1977; Epic 8-50403; chart high No.59.

**'Seaside Woman' (Linda McCartney)**
Linda McCartney (keyboards, vocals), Paul McCartney (bass), Denny Laine (guitar), Henry McCulloch (guitar), Denny Seiwell (drums). Recorded at AIR Studios, London, England.
**'B Side To Seaside' (McCartney)**
Linda McCartney (vocals), Paul McCartney (bass, drums, guitar, keyboards). Recorded at Abbey Road Studios, London, England. Both produced by Paul McCartney.

'SEASIDE WOMAN'
Written in 1971, recorded in 1973, issued in 1977 'Seaside Woman' was Linda McCartney's first solo vinyl outing and a fun one at that. The McCartneys loved reggae but, like John Lennon, McCartney struggled to get white musicians to play with any kind of empathy for the music. One has only to compare Wings' attempt at reggae with the two songs cut by Lee 'Scratch' Perry for Linda in the summer of 1977 to hear just how clumsy they were. (The Perry cuts were 'Mr Sandman' and 'Sugartime', later modified, and released on the posthumous Linda collection *Wide Prairie* in 1998). That aside, 'Seaside Woman' is a fun pop song that should have faired better in the charts, particularly in Britain where there was a large audience for reggae in all its variations.

Like previous side-projects, 'Seaside Woman' was issued using a pseudonym. Linda explained: "When we were in Jamaica, there had been a fantastic reggae version of 'Suzi Q', so they used to call me Suzi. And the beer in Jamaica is called Red Stripe, so that makes it Suzi and the Red Stripes." By the mid 1970s, McCartney had the idea of recording an album's worth of material in New York using the Suzy And The Red Stripes pseudonym. What exactly he had in mind is unclear, and the proposed project never materialised.

McCartney wrote the aptly named 'B Side To Seaside' in Africa in 1973 but did not record it until March 1977. He played all the instruments and Linda sang lead and backing vocals.

**'Seaside Woman' data**
In the USA, Epic issued a mono/stereo 7-inch demonstration single (8-50403) on red or black vinyl. They also issued a black vinyl 12-inch demonstration single (XSS 163108). Commercial copies of the Epic release were issued on 7-inch black vinyl with genetic Epic labels and paper sleeve.

In Britain, A&M issued a yellow vinyl edition of the single with customised red and yellow labels in a glossy sleeve with red and white diagonal stripes, with the title top centre and the artist's name bottom right. The single was also released in a presentation 10-inch by 8-inch box that included 'saucy' seaside postcards and a badge. A&M issued a demonstration single on black vinyl with generic labels with a large 'A' at the centre of the label with 'PROMOTIONAL COPY NOT FOR SALE' on two lines below.

## 'MULL OF KINTYRE' / 'GIRLS' SCHOOL'
## WINGS
**UK release** November 11 1977; Capitol R 6018; chart high No.1.
**US release** November 14 1977; Capitol 4504; chart high No.33.

### 'Mull Of Kintyre' (McCartney, Laine)
Paul McCartney (guitar, vocals), Linda McCartney (backing vocals), Denny Laine (guitar, backing vocals), Joe English (drums), The Campbelltown Pipe Band (pipes). Recorded on RAK Mobile Studio at Spirit Of Ranachan Studio, High Park Farm, Scotland, and at AIR Studios and Abbey Road Studios, London, England.
### 'Girls' School' (McCartney)
Paul McCartney (bass, backing vocals), Linda McCartney (keyboards, backing vocals), Denny Laine (guitar, backing vocals), Jimmy McCulloch (guitar), Joe English (drums). Recorded at Abbey Road Studios, London.
Both produced by Paul McCartney.

'MULL OF KINTYRE'
Love it or loath it, 'Mull Of Kintyre' was a massive hit and Wings' bestselling single, ever. If there were any doubts about Wings popularity, 'Mull Of Kintyre' should have put paid to them when it overtook 'She Loves You', which had held the record as the bestselling single in Britain for 14 years.

Musically, the song is hardly typical of McCartney or Wings, but it does typify his fondness for romanticism. McCartney first made a piano based demo of the song sometime in 1974. This work in progress version was taken at a slightly slower tempo and lacked a finished lyric, McCartney filling in the blanks with some ad-libs. Work on the song continued with help from Denny Laine and Tony Wilson, Pipe Major with the Campbeltown Pipe Band, who instructed him about the keys in which bagpipes can play. Once he'd finished the song, he recorded an acoustic guitar based demo with Denny Laine providing harmonies and keyboards.

Well aware that it would attract adverse criticism, McCartney at one point considered holding the single back. "I nearly didn't put it out – and that's a fact," he explained. "I knew old folks, Scottish people and The Campbelltown Pipers liked it ... but at that time it seemed that everything was punk. ... But you can't not release records because someone is gonna slag it ... you just go along with your instincts and hope that you're right." His gamble paid off: the record's anthemic qualities crossed boundaries of generation and taste. Punk may have given the finger to rock's elder statesmen, but the old-garde maintained its hegemony over the young pretenders, and sales of 'Mull Of Kintyre' were more than healthy.

A song about McCartney's fondness for the Scottish countryside, 'Mull Of Kintyre' was inspired by the rural setting he has enjoyed since buying a farm there in the mid 1960s. Speaking on Radio 1 to Mike Read, he said: "The thing about 'Mull Of Kintyre' was John had given me a sort of love of Scotland, and I'd eventually got a farm up there ... and I'd got to really like the place." Linda confirmed the McCartneys' love of the country. "Scotland was like nothing I'd ever lived in. It was the most beautiful land you have ever seen – it was way at the end of nowhere."

McCartney wanted to write about this part of Scotland, but also to write a song with a contemporary Scottish feel. "Being up there, I'd sort of heard some bagpipe music and stuff, it's very nice … but it's all old," he said. "I couldn't relate to it and I thought, much as I like it, it would be nice if there was a sort of newer Scottish song. So I thought, 'Oh well, I'll try and write one.'" McCartney's Scottish ballad successfully evoked the kind of romantic idealism associated with Sir Edwin Landseer's *Monarch Of The Glen* and Burns' vernacular poetry to great effect, gave it a modern twist and captured the public imagination more successfully than any other Wings single.

The finished song was recorded on the McCartneys' farm in the grandly named Spirit Of Ranachan Studios, a converted barn equipped with RAK's 24-track mobile studio. The backing track of guitars, snare drums, and bagpipes was recorded one August evening and remixed later in London. Jimmy McCulloch had by now quit the band and so doesn't feature, but Joe English does. Although Wings had almost completed their forthcoming album, *London Town*, on return to Britain in the summer of 1977, McCulloch announced that he was leaving to join the reformed Small Faces (probably around early September).

Although McCartney was reluctant to go into any detail about McCulloch's departure, it's obvious that relations between the two had been tense. "Jimmy leaving was a very complicated thing, but I think basically he didn't want to be committed to any group for too long a period when he joined," McCartney said. "Then he was offered the gig with The Small Faces, which he really fancied. We'd had what you might call one or two bad patches, and it seemed to make sense to call it quits."

English left soon after that, joining Sea Level, a band fronted by piano player and session musician Chuck Leavell, and later putting together his own Christian rock group, The Joe English Band.

The B-side, 'Girls' School', offered something a little less esoteric for those whose taste didn't run to bagpipes and Scottish ballads. McCartney chose it as the flip precisely because it represented the band's "more rocking side". He wrote it in the late summer of 1976, while on holiday in Hawaii, inspired by advertisements for pornographic films. "I was looking through one of those American newspapers and the back page, at the end of the entertainment section, is always like the porno films," he said. "I rather liked the titles, so basically I took all the titles and made a song out of them. For example, there was a film called *School Mistress*, another called *Curly Haired*, one called *Kid Sister*, and another called *The Woman Trainer*, and I liked those titles so much I just wove them into a song."

'Girls' School' was recorded in February 1977 at Abbey Road and is a heads-down-no-nonsense-rocker; as such it was favoured by American DJs over the quaint 'Mull Of Kintyre'. Even so, 'Girls' School' was a relative flop there, managing only number 33 in the *Billboard* charts. (The edit of 'Girls' School', issued on demonstration copies of the single, later appeared as the bonus track on the first pressing of the *London Town* CD, the remastered edition features the full-length version.)

### 'Mull Of Kintyre' data

'Mull Of Kintyre' was issued with Capitol 'dome' labels and a picture sleeve. To promote the single, Capitol issued radio stations with edits of A and B-sides. American (SPRO-8746) and British (R 6018 [7YCE. 21798–DJ]) demonstration singles were issued with black and silver Capitol 'dome' labels.

The single was issued with two label variations in America: black and silver Capitol 'dome' labels or 'purple' Capitol labels.

The single was promoted with three different videos, each showing Paul, Linda, Denny, and The Campbelltown Pipers miming to the song, either in a studio or on location in and around the Mull of Kintyre. In addition, Wings appeared on *The Mike Yarwood Christmas Show* in a sketch with the comedian and miming to the song.

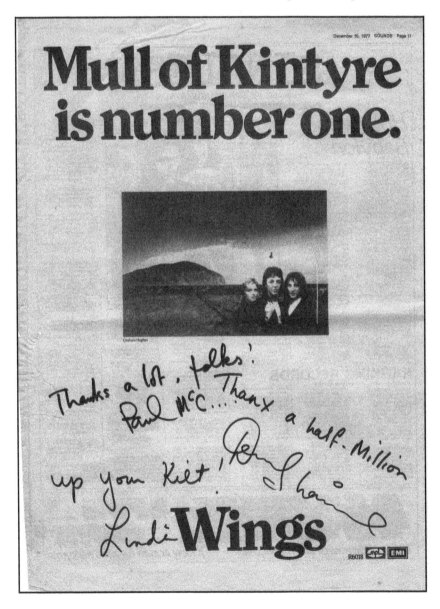

Blue and orange vinyl editions issued in Israel.

Irish Parlophone issue

# MULL OF KINTYRE

## WINGS DOUBLE A

# GIRLS SCHOOL

1978: With A Little Luck to Wings Greatest

'WITH A LITTLE LUCK' / 'BACKWARDS TRAVELLER / CUFF LINK'
WINGS
**UK release** March 23 1978; Parlophone R 6019; chart high No.5.
**US release** March 20 1978; Capitol 4559; chart high No.1.

### 'With A Little Luck' (McCartney)
Paul McCartney (bass, keyboards, vocals), Linda McCartney (keyboards, backing vocals), Denny Laine (guitar, backing vocal), Jimmy McCulloch (guitar, backing vocal), Joe English (drums). Mobile studio recording aboard motor-yacht Fair Carol.
### 'Backwards Traveller / Cuff Link' (McCartney)
Paul McCartney (bass, guitar, keyboards, drums, vocals), Linda McCartney (backing vocals), Denny Laine (guitar, backing vocals). Recorded at Abbey Road Studios and AIR Studios, London, England.
Both produced by Paul McCartney.

'WITH A LITTLE LUCK'
McCartney wrote 'With A Little Luck' on his farm in Scotland, and the song was recorded by Wings at Watermelon Bay in the Virgin Islands, aboard the yacht Fair Carol. The song remained unfinished until completed at Abbey Road in late autumn 1977, by which time Jimmy McCulloch and Joe English had left the group.

Relying on remarkably thin-sounding keyboards, the song's dilute, synthetic tone ironically echoes McCartney's equally unimaginative lyric. McCartney's irritating optimism, both musically and lyrically, appears functional at best as 'With A Little Luck' lacks the unexpected melodic twists and turns that mark McCartney at his best. An over-reliance on synthetic instrumentation combined with a too-finely tuned sense of studio craftsmanship effectively negates any semblance of atmosphere or character.

Unfortunately, the more McCartney attempted to make his records sound effortless, the more they appeared suffused with artifice. Compounded by laborious overdubbing, which effectively distanced the band from any sense of performance and unity, 'With A Little Luck' is little more than writing by numbers and sadly predictable. It was, however, a US Number 1, which probably say more about the state of the American music industry at the time than anything about this Wings single.

'Backwards Traveller/Cuff Link' was recorded by Paul, Linda, and Denny Laine at Abbey Road in the last week of October 1977 and completed in January the following year. With McCulloch and English absent, McCartney played drums, bass, acoustic guitar, and keyboards. It's a medley of two songs: 'Backwards Traveller' is a typical McCartney pot-boiler and 'Cuff Link' an uninspired instrumental.

### 'With A Little Luck' data
The single was issued with customised 'London Town' labels, which were used for every release associated with the London Town album. To promote the single, an edit of the A-side – with the lengthy instrumental coda removed – was issued to radio stations. American copies of the demonstration single (PRO-8812) were issued with mono/stereo edits. British copies of the demonstration single were issued with 'A side DJ' above the catalogue number with the stereo edit on the A-side and the full-length version on the B-side (the edit was later used for the Wingspan compilation album).

*LONDON TOWN*
WINGS
**Side 1** 'London Town', 'Cafe On The Left Bank', 'I'm Carrying', 'Backwards Traveller', 'Cuff Link', 'Children Children', 'Girlfriend', 'I've Had Enough'.
**Side 2** 'With A Little Luck', 'Famous Groupies', 'Deliver Your Children', 'Name And Address', 'Don't Let It Bring You Down', 'Morse Moose And The Grey Goose'.
**UK release** March 31 1978; Parlophone PAS 10012; chart high No.4.
**US release** March 27 1978; LP Capitol SW-11777; 8-track cartridge Capitol 8XW-1177; chart high No.2.

**'London Town' (McCartney, Laine)**
Paul McCartney (bass, keyboards, vocals), Linda McCartney (keyboards, backing vocals), Denny Laine (guitar, backing vocal), Jimmy McCulloch (guitar, backing vocal), Joe English (drums).
**'Cafe On The Left Bank' (McCartney)**
Personnel as 'London Town'.
**'I'm Carrying' (McCartney)**
Paul McCartney (guitar, Gizmo, vocals).
**'Children Children' (Laine, McCartney)**
Paul McCartney (bass, guitar, keyboards, violin, autoharp, recorder, backing vocals), Linda McCartney (backing vocals), Denny Laine (guitar, recorder, vocals).
**'Girlfriend' (McCartney)**
Paul McCartney (bass, guitar, keyboards, drums, vocals), Linda McCartney (backing vocals), Denny Laine (guitar, backing vocals).
**'I've Had Enough' (McCartney)**
Personnel as 'London Town' except Jimmy McCulloch (guitar).
**'Famous Groupies' (McCartney)**
Personnel as 'London Town' except Jimmy McCulloch (guitar).
**'Deliver Your Children' (Laine, McCartney)**
Paul McCartney (bass, guitar, backing vocals), Linda McCartney (backing vocals), Denny Laine (guitar, vocals).
**'Name And Address' (McCartney)**
Personnel as 'Deliver Your Children'.
**'Don't Let It Bring You Down' (McCartney, Laine)**
Paul McCartney (bass, flageolet, vocals), Linda McCartney (backing vocals), Denny Laine (guitar, flageolet, backing vocal), Jimmy McCulloch (guitar), Joe English (drums).
**'Morse Moose And The Grey Goose' (McCartney, Laine)**
Paul McCartney (bass, Mellotron, vocals), Linda McCartney (keyboards, backing vocals), Denny Laine (guitar, keyboards, backing vocal), Jimmy McCulloch (guitar), Joe English (drums).
All recorded on Mobile Studio aboard motor-yacht Fair Carol, Virgin Islands, and at AIR Studios, London, England, except: 'London Town' recorded at Abbey Road Studios, London; 'Children, Children', 'Girlfriend', 'Deliver Your Children, 'Name And Address' recorded at Abbey Road Studios and AIR Studios, London. All produced by Paul McCartney.

## LONDON TOWN

After the frenetic work schedule of the previous two years, McCartney decided to take a leisurely approach to recording Wings' next album, *London Town*. Linda was pregnant, again, and as she was an integral part of the band, Wings would be taking it easy for the next 12 months. Any momentum Wings had was effectively lost because McCartney, quite rightly, didn't want to place Linda under any more stress than was necessary. After completing their world tour in October 1976, Wings took a three-month break before beginning work on a new album on February 7 1977 at Abbey Road. The sleevenotes suggest that sessions continued uninterrupted from early February until the end of March, but on February 20, Paul and Linda left Britain for Jamaica and a two-week holiday. Recording recommenced on their return before stopping again at the end of March. In early May, Wings moved to Watermelon Bay, Virgin Islands, where they recorded aboard the motor-yacht Fair Carol.

It was Denny Laine who hit on the idea of recording aboard a boat. He had lived on a houseboat, *Searchlight*, for a number of years, and a visit to a floating studio in Los Angeles convinced him it was a good idea. Recording aboard a floating studio sounds idyllic, but the trip was not without incident. McCartney and Jimmy McCulloch suffered injuries to their knees, falling and cutting them badly, and sound engineer Geoff Emerick electrocuted his foot. McCulloch also managed to go deaf in one ear, which must have been something of a handicap when it came to recording. If these minor irritations weren't enough, US Customs officials, searching for marijuana, raided the three yachts McCartney had hired for the trip. Although no action was taken against any member of Wings or the crew, they did receive an official warning.

During their four-week stay in the Virgin Islands, Wings recorded nine songs, seven of which found their way onto the finished album ('Waterspout' and Laine's 'Find A Way' did not make it). The group then returned to the UK, where, after another break, recording recommenced on October 25, probably to finish work on 'Mull Of Kintyre'.

By now McCulloch and English had quit the band and Wings Mk.6 were down to a three-piece: Paul, Linda, and Denny Laine. They spent five weeks at Abbey Road before switching to AIR, also in London, for 12 days in December, and then in January 1978 returned to Abbey Road for a further three weeks to finish the album.

*London Town* represents another defining moment — not because of musical excellence, but because during the 12 months in which the album was compiled, Wings returned once again to the McCartney–Laine–McCartney core. Although Paul hoped that Wings would emulate the kind of democracy he'd enjoyed with The Beatles, the balancing act required to keep a group together became too much. Speaking to the *NME* in 1978, he said: "From the very beginning, I never intended that Wings should be me and anyone would do to play back-up. But as to why there have been changes .... Look, when you've been in bands, when you've been through all the hassles ... how can I put it? You reach a point where you realise you don't need a situation where, if someone is a brilliant player but just being around him gets to be obnoxious ... who needs it! I'm not saying that's the reason why we've had so many personnel changes in Wings, all I'm saying is that you've gotta feel right together and enjoy one another's company."

Not for the first time, Wings were in trouble. When McCullough and Seiwell had left on the eve of recording a new album, *Band On The Run*, McCartney had appeared resigned to the loss of these musicians. This time, the guitarist and drummer left while recording was in progress, and the departure of McCulloch and English had a more profound effect. McCartney's dissatisfaction was clearly audible in the music he recorded.

*London Town* was a disappointment. Even McCartney admitted as much. Speaking immediately after its release, he said: "I'd like to make an adventurous album, and we're discussing the possibilities of doing just that, for the hell of it. No formula style … I'd welcome the change … [I] love having fun with the music instead of getting my head down and thinking along the lines of: I am Led Zeppelin and I've got to come out with something heavy because that's what they expect of me."

Despite the departure of McCulloch and English during its recording, McCartney still managed to record Wings' most successful single ever, 'Mull Of Kintyre', and most successful album since *Band On The Run*. *London Town* out performed *At The Speed Of Sound* thanks to massive sales in Germany, Holland, Belgium, Italy, and Norway.

### London Town songs

McCartney's jet-set lifestyle meant that many of the songs on *London Town* were written while he was on the road or on holiday. The album's opening track was written in November 1975 while Wings were in Perth, Australia completing the first leg of their world tour. Written with Denny Laine, 'London Town' was completed in Scotland between touring commitments. McCartney presents a romanticised view of London: part reportage and part fantasy, his description of the sprawling metropolis fuses idealisation with acute observations of everyday street life. Recorded with Wings Mk.5, it was one of the first songs completed for the album.

If 'London Town' was a well observed albeit idealised view of the nation's capital, 'Cafe On The Left Bank' was an equally pointed piece of observation about the English abroad. Recorded on the group's first day at Watermelon Bay, the song has more of a buzz to it than other songs recorded there, perhaps a consequence of it being recorded before the band slipped into holiday mode. One of the stronger tracks on the album, it's saved by McCulloch's robust playing.

'I'm Carrying' was recorded on May 5 aboard the Fair Carol and features McCartney playing acoustic guitar, double-tracked throughout. The string section was over-dubbed in London, where McCartney also added an electric guitar part played with a Gizmo, a small handheld device for guitar that vibrates rather than plucks the strings, making for a sustained tone, which was combined with the orchestral strings. 'I'm Carrying' is a gentle ballad that restates much of what McCartney had expressed with 'Yesterday' – less adventurous melodically, but no less welcoming.

The first of two vocal contributions from Laine, 'Children Children' was inspired in part by a small waterfall in McCartney's garden. At the time of its writing, Laine was missing his children and was "preoccupied by those kind of themes." Co-written with McCartney, 'Children Children' was originally titled 'Laine And Heidi' until McCartney suggested the new title, as he thought the original too sentimental. Recorded by the McCartney–Laine–McCartney line-up, it features McCartney and Laine on recorders and McCartney on violin.

'Girlfriend' is by far the most commercially successful song on the album, thanks to Michael Jackson, and is an odd mix of soul ballad (chorus and verses) and pop song (middle eight and instrumental). Jackson would record the song for his multimillion selling *Off The Wall* album and suggested that it was written specifically for him. McCartney wrote 'Girlfriend' while on holiday in Switzerland and recorded a demo in November 1974, which would place it in circulation at the time the two stars first met. But McCartney denies writing the song for Jackson. Nevertheless, on its release, McCartney wondered what the singer might make of it and made light-hearted references to it sounding like The Jackson Five, so the idea of having Jackson record it may have been on his mind for some time. However, it was only once Wings recorded 'Girlfriend' that Jackson, at the insistence of his producer, Quincy Jones, decided to attempt the song himself. One reason for it sounding like Jackson is McCartney's uncharacteristic falsetto, which is backed by equally high harmonies from Laine and Linda.

'I've Had Enough' was recorded by Wings Mk.5 in the Virgin Islands. Despite a half-decent riff and a snappy arrangement with dramatic stabs and accents, like much of the material on *London Town* it lacks punch. The song evolved from a jam session with McCartney improvising the chorus. "We recorded it on the boat ... but we still didn't have any words until we got back to London," he explained, "and then I wrote a few. I overdubbed the vocals in London, and it's just one of those 'fed-up' songs."

If Wings were recording in a holiday atmosphere, why was it that all McCartney could come up with was a chorus as negative as 'I've Had Enough'? Perhaps it reflects his attitude toward the band. Maybe relations within the group had already disintegrated, for it would appear that even when 'having fun' they were merely going through the motions.

'Famous Groupies' relates the tales of various fictitious musicians and roadies, not to mention groupies, and their exploits. McCartney wrote it in Scotland and recorded it in the Virgin Islands. Originally an up-tempo rocker, it was given a relaxed treatment that fits the album's pedestrian mood. McCartney could have drawn on a lifetime of experience to write this song and it could have been a real exposé of life on the road, yet he opted for a humorous fantasy narrative – perhaps to protect the innocent and his own squeaky-clean reputation. Another of McCartney's 'comedy' songs, 'Famous Groupies' fails to raise much of a laugh or to achieve much musically.

Denny Laine began writing 'Deliver Your Children' while Wings were recording *Venus And Mars*. McCartney helped complete the song, which was held over for *London Town*. Delivered up-tempo with a bright acoustic backing, its only weakness is a lyric that, although far from the worst on the album, tends to ramble from one theme to another.

'Name And Address' is a reworking of 1950s rock'n'roll and finds McCartney attempting to pay homage to the heroes of his youth. Like many musicians of his generation, he owed a huge debt to American rock'n'roll and Elvis Presley in particular. As he explained to Roy Carr, 'Name And Address' is "an Elvisy-type thing and not a screaming Little Richard-type track. It's held back". He wasn't wrong: 'Name And Address' is so held back it's almost comatose. This is rock'n'roll with its slippers on. It was recorded in London with McCartney on drums, bass, and lead guitar, and its only redeeming feature is its directness, which, in comparison with much of what appeared on the album, makes it sound surprisingly fresh.

McCartney's resolute optimism struck again in the form of 'Don't Let It Bring You Down', a mid-tempo ballad written over a two-year period. He started the song while on tour in Scotland in 1975. "I think we were in Aberdeen, sitting in our hotel bedroom, just before we were going to turn in for the night, and I had my 12-string guitar with me. I started plonking out a little tune and it became 'Don't Let It Bring You Down'." The song's sanguine lyric is complimented by a pleasing see-saw melody that echoes the rise and fall of the fatalistic theme, which can be read as the musical equivalent of McCartney's apparent belief in eternal recurrence. McCartney and Laine added flageolets (Irish tin whistles), which alternate with McCulloch's warm fuzz-tone guitar. Combined, they suggest both a sense of place and an air of resigned fatalism.

While aboard the Fair Carol, McCartney and Laine began to experiment with an electric piano. McCartney played a series of unrelated notes that suggested Morse code while Laine occasionally gave the instrument a thump. This piece of atonal experimentation was recorded and formed the basis of 'Morse Moose And The Grey Goose'. Using this as a 'bed', McCartney laid down a funky bass riff, while the rest of the band contributed a few dramatic stabs to add some much-needed verve. That's how the track remained until Wings returned to Britain. The song's countermelody, lyric, Mellotron, acoustic guitars, and vocals were added in London. 'Morse Moose And The Grey Goose' is a well developed jam that had a considerable amount of work done to it, but it remains little more than a pot-boiler and is accordingly flimsy.

### London Town data
The album was issued with customised labels, printed inner sleeve, and a large 33-inch by 23-inch double-sided poster – with Jimmy McCulloch and Joe English conspicuous by their absence. Capitol issued the album on 8-track (8XW 11777). EMI issued the album on CD (CD-FA 3223) on August 29 1989 and issued a remastered edition (CDPMCOL8) on July 7 1993. Capitol issued the CD (CDP 7 48198 2) on June 20 1989.

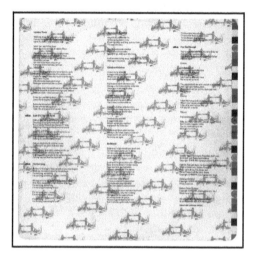

London Town poster

## 'I'VE HAD ENOUGH' / 'DELIVER YOUR CHILDREN'
### WINGS
**UK release** June 16 1978; Parlophone R 6020; chart high No.42.
**US release** June 5 1978; Capitol 4594; chart high No.25.

### 'I'VE HAD ENOUGH'
Parlophone issued 'I've Had Enough' with customised labels and a picture sleeve. Promotional copies were issued with a large 'A' above the spindle hole and 'DEMO RECORD NOT FOR SALE' on three lines below.

Capitol issued the single with customised labels but without a picture sleeve, and issued a mono/stereo demonstration single (P-4595) with customised labels and a press release.

## LONDON TOWN' / 'I'M CARRYING'
### WINGS
**UK release** August 11 1978; Parlophone R 6021; chart high No.60.
**US release** August 14 1978; Capitol 4625; chart high No.39.

### 'LONDON TOWN'
Parlophone issued 'London Town' with customised labels and a plain paper sleeve. Promotional copies were issued with a large 'A' above the spindle hole and 'DEMO RECORD NOT FOR SALE' on three lines below.

The Capitol issue matched the British release, but Capitol also issued a mono/stereo demonstration single (P-4625).

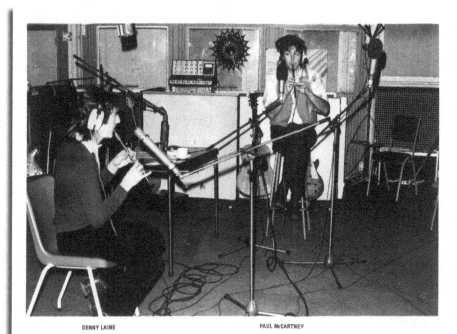

DENNY LAINE          PAUL McCARTNEY

**WINGS**

# LONDON TOWN SINGLE

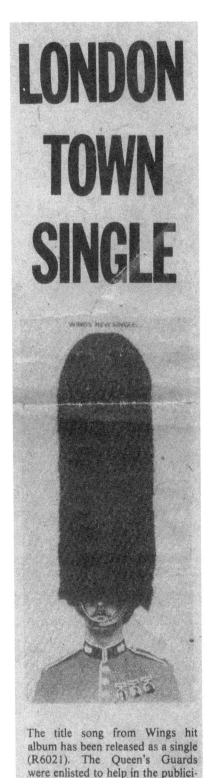

The title song from Wings hit album has been released as a single (R6021). The Queen's Guards were enlisted to help in the publicity as this poster shows.

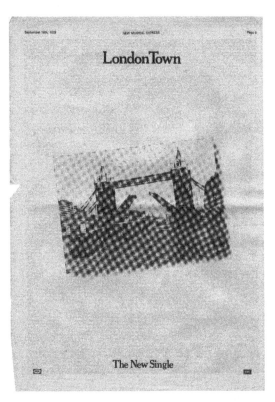

## LondonTown

### The New Single

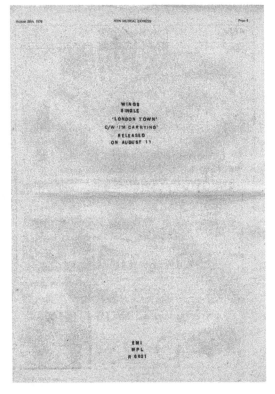

WINGS
SINGLE
'LONDON TOWN'
C/W 'I'M CARRYING'
RELEASED
ON AUGUST 11

EMI
MPL
R 6021

## WINGS GREATEST
## WINGS

**Side 1** 'Another Day', 'Silly Love Songs', 'Live And Let Die', 'Junior's Farm', 'With A Little Luck', 'Band On The Run'.
**Side 2** 'Uncle Albert/Admiral Halsey', 'Hi, Hi, Hi', 'Let 'Em In', 'My Love', 'Jet', 'Mull Of Kintyre'.
**UK release** December 1 1978; Parlophone PCTC 256; chart high No.3.
**US release** November 27 1978; LP Capitol SOO-11905; 8-track cartridge Capitol 8XOO-11905; chart high No.29.
For personnel, recording locations, and producer credits see original entries.

WINGS GREATEST
Although Wings had consistently fared better in America than in Britain, this first best-of sold better in the UK. Compiled with British and American markets in mind, *Wings Greatest* was probably produced to fulfil contractual agreements. McCartney had recently signed with Columbia in America and so may have owed EMI/Capitol an album before departing for his new label.

The sleeve was designed by Paul and Linda with assistance from Hipgnosis and was photographed at considerable expense by Angus Forbes. McCartney arranged for an art deco statuette to be flown to Switzerland and photographed on the Matterhorn – thus more money was spent on the cover of this record than some bands were spending on recording entire new albums.

The album was issued with customised labels (black, with the statuette top centre) and a 30-inch by 20-inch poster of Wings Mk.6. Capitol issued the album on 8-track cartridge (8XOO 11905). EMI issued the CD (CDP7460562) on February 4 1985 and Capitol on December 1 1986.

1979: Goodnight Tonight to Wonderful Christmastime

## 'GOODNIGHT TONIGHT' / 'DAYTIME NIGHTIME SUFFERING'
## WINGS
**UK release** March 23 1979; Parlophone R 6023; 12-inch Parlophone 12Y R 6023; chart high No.5.
**US release** March 19 1979; Columbia 3-10939; 12-inch Columbia 23-10940; chart high No.5.

### 'Goodnight Tonight' (McCartney)
Paul McCartney (bass, drums, keyboards, vocals), Linda McCartney (keyboards, backing vocals), Denny Laine (guitar, backing vocals), Laurence Juber (guitar, backing vocals), Steve Holly (percussion). Recorded at Abbey Road Studios and Replica Studio, London, England. Produced by Paul McCartney.
### 'Daytime Nightime Suffering' (McCartney)
Paul McCartney (bass, keyboards, vocals), Linda McCartney (keyboards, backing vocals), Denny Laine (guitar, backing vocals), Laurence Juber (guitar, backing vocals), Steve Holly (drums). Recorded at Replica Studio and Abbey Road. Produced by Paul McCartney and Chris Thomas.

### 'GOODNIGHT TONIGHT'
McCartney originally recorded 'Goodnight Tonight' as a solo project when sessions for *London Town* came to a close. It then sat on the shelf for almost a year, because he was unsure whether or not it would make a good single. Speaking to *Rolling Stone* just after its release, he said: "'Goodnight Tonight' was going to be the B-side and 'Daytime Nightime Suffering' was going to be the A-side. So we sat around for years – well, it seemed like years – discussing it, you know? The normal soul searching you go through. And we decided no, it isn't all right, we won't put it out. And about a week later, I played the record again. I thought, 'That's crazy, we've made it; it's stupid, why not put it out?' So we decided to do it."

Overdubbed during sessions for *Back To The Egg*, it was left off the album but became Wings' third bestselling single. A pop song pure and simple, 'Goodnight Tonight' had toes tapping, possessed an infectious chorus, and sounded great on the dance floor. Which is often all that's needed.

A favourite of McCartney's, 'Daytime Nightime Suffering' was recorded at Replica Studio, a copy of Abbey Road's Number Two studio situated in the basement of his MPL offices in Soho, London. The band were mixing *Back To The Egg* and due to finish for the week when McCartney challenged everyone to write a song over the weekend, the best to be recorded for possible inclusion on the album. New drummer Steve Holly recalled: "So we all went off and we individually wrote songs. I can't remember quite what it was that I did. I did do a couple of tunes. And, of course, we played our songs, our best efforts from the weekend, one after the other. And then Paul said, 'Well, I wrote this,' and played 'Daytime Nightime Suffering'. Well, it's easy to see who won the competition."

The song features some sensational vocal harmonies and one of the best lead vocals that McCartney had delivered in some time. Its uncluttered arrangement and meticulous production (remixed 49 times before McCartney was satisfied) benefits one of his strongest B-sides.

Like Sandy Povey's 'Born A Woman', Helen Reddy's 'I Am Woman', or even John Lennon's 'Woman Is The Nigger Of The World', 'Daytime Nightime Suffering' was meant as a celebration of womanhood. "[That's] a pro-women song," McCartney recalled. "'What does she get for all of this?' Daytime nightime suffering. It's like the plight of women." Whatever its merits as a piece of pro-feminist dogma, it's a fine pop song.

### Goodnight Tonight data

This was the first Wings single to be issued in Britain with generic Parlophone labels and was also their first UK 12-inch single. The 7-inch was issued with a plain paper sleeve; the 12-inch with a 1950s-style inner sleeve and laminated picture cover. Promotional copies of the 7-inch single were issued with a large 'A' at 10 o'clock and 'DEMO RECORD NOT FOR SALE' on three lines above the spindle hole.

In the USA, Columbia followed the British release, issuing both 7 and 12-inch singles with generic labels, the 12-inch with either a picture or generic sleeve. Columbia issued a mono demonstration 7-inch single (3-10939) with white labels with black text and the large Columbia logo in red, top centre. They also issued a demonstration 12-inch (23-10940) with white labels with black text, with the long and short stereo mixes on either side of the disc. In 1980, Columbia reissued 'Goodnight Tonight' (13-33405) with 'Getting Closer' on their Hall Of Fame imprint.

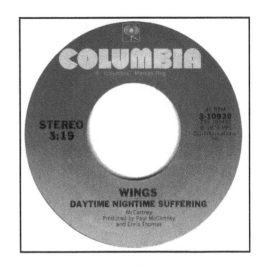

'OLD SIAM, SIR' / 'SPIN IT ON'
WINGS
**UK release** June 1 1979; Parlophone R 6026; chart high No.35.

### 'Old Siam, Sir' (McCartney)
### 'Spin It On' (McCartney)
Both with Paul McCartney (bass, keyboards, vocals), Linda McCartney (keyboards, backing vocals), Denny Laine (guitar, backing vocals), Laurence Juber (guitar), Steve Holly (drums). Both recorded on RAK Mobile Studio at Spirit of Ranachan Studio, Scotland. Both produced by Paul McCartney and Chris Thomas.

### 'Old Siam, Sir'
While 'Goodnight Tonight' had explored the contemporary fascination with dance music, 'Old Siam, Sir' / 'Spin It On' offered gritty slices of abrasive ROCK. With punk and new wave in ascendance, McCartney responded with some of the rawest material he'd recorded in years. His musical tastes have always been eclectic, and as he told *Musician* magazine immediately after the release of *Back To The Egg*, it ranged from "Fred Astaire to The Sex Pistols". For McCartney, punk/new wave marked a return to the kind of musical primitivism expressed by rock'n'roll's originators. "The nice thing about new wave is that its got back to real music, rather than pop," he said.

McCartney had of course spent much of the 1970s exploring his pop sensibilities and distancing himself from 'real music'. One could argue that he'd been responsible for many of the worst crimes committed in the name of pop and epitomised many of the values that punk/new wave now railed against. But Wings' new sound wasn't a rejection of one style in favour of another, or a desperate attempt to appear to be in touch with the kids; rather, it combined pop sensibilities with a new-wave rush.

Linda developed the riff for 'Old Siam, Sir' while rehearsing, and McCartney and Laine completed it later. McCartney added a lyric about a girl returning to Britain from Siam before recording a solo demo, titled 'Super Big Heatwave', at Rude Studio (a permanent well-appointed 4-track demo studio that McCartney installed at his Scottish farm in the early 1970s). Much of the lyric was improvised, but he decided to keep his nonsense verse for no other reason than because it "kinda stuck". Never one to over-analyse his writing, McCartney often prefers to leave his original ideas un-changed. It's not clear if this is due to laziness or superstition – he may be afraid of loosing the 'magic' that he believes is somehow bound to the songwriting process – but it too often leads to substandard material. With a little more attention, 'Old Siam, Sir' might have been saved. Yet despite Paul, Linda, and Denny having a hand in its writing, it's an uninspired if gritty rocker.

Another rocker, 'Spin It On' was recorded in one day, July 23 1978, and was the last song recorded during the *Back To The Egg* sessions held at McCartney's Scottish farm.

### 'Old Siam, Sir' data
Parlophone issued 'Old Siam, Sir' / 'Spin It On' with customised 'egg' labels and custom die-cut sleeve. Demo copies have 'DEMO RECORD NOT FOR SALE' on three lines above the spindle hole and a large 'A' below the spindle hole.

'GETTING CLOSER' / 'SPIN IT ON'
WINGS
**US release** June 11 1979; Columbia 3-11020; chart high No.20.

### 'Getting Closer' (McCartney)
Paul McCartney (bass, keyboards, vocals), Linda McCartney (keyboards, backing vocals), Denny Laine (guitar, backing vocals), Laurence Juber (guitar), Steve Holly (drums). Recorded at Abbey Road Studios, London, England. Produced by Paul McCartney and Chris Thomas.

### 'GETTING CLOSER'
McCartney began writing 'Getting Closer' in 1974 and recorded a piano-based demo with an unfinished middle-eight some time that year. Dropping the middle-eight and increasing the tempo, Wings transformed the song into an energetic rocker. The band recorded the basic track, with Laine and McCartney singing alternative verses, at Abbey Road in October 1978. Influenced by the previous week's recording session with Rockestra, McCartney overdubbed numerous guitar parts to create a dense sonic aura. The song was completed at Replica Studio in March 1979 with keyboard overdubs and an edit.

### 'Getting Closer' data
Issued in the USA, Europe, and Japan in favour of 'Old Siam, Sir', 'Getting Closer' performed better in America than its British counterpart. Issued with a die-cut sleeve, the single was issued by Columbia with generic labels. Columbia issued a mono/stereo demonstration single with white labels with black text, and the large Columbia logo in red, top centre of the label. Columbia later reissued 'Getting Closer' (13-33405) on their Hall Of Fame imprint, backed with 'Goodnight Tonight'.

*BACK TO THE EGG*
WINGS
**Side 1** 'Reception', 'Getting Closer', 'We're Open Tonight', 'Spin It On', 'Again And Again And Again', 'Old Siam, Sir', 'Arrow Through Me'.
**Side 2** 'Rockestra Theme', 'After The Ball', 'Million Miles', 'Winter Rose', 'Love Awake ', 'The Broadcast', 'So Glad To See You Here', 'Baby's Request'.
**UK release** June 8 1979; Parlophone PCTC 257; chart high No.4.
**US release** June 11 1979; LP Columbia FC-36057; 8-track cartridge Columbia FCA-36057; chart high No.8.

**'Reception' (McCartney)**
Paul McCartney (bass, keyboards), Linda McCartney (keyboards), Denny Laine (guitar), Laurence Juber (guitar), Steve Holly (drums), Mrs Margary (recitation). Mobile Studio recording at Lympne Castle, Hythe, Kent, England.
**'We're Open Tonight' (McCartney)**
Paul McCartney (guitar, vocals), Laurence Juber (12-string guitar). Mobile Studio recording at Lympne Castle.
**'Again And Again And Again' (Laine)**
Paul McCartney (bass, keyboards, backing vocals), Linda McCartney (keyboards, backing vocals), Denny Laine (guitar, vocals), Laurence Juber (guitar), Steve Holly (drums). Recorded on RAK Mobile Studio at Spirit Of Ranachan Studio, Scotland.
**'Arrow Through Me' (McCartney)**
Paul McCartney (bass, Moog, Fender Rhodes electric piano, Clavinet, vocals), Linda McCartney (backing vocals), Steve Holly (drums). Recorded at Spirit Of Ranachan Studio, and at Replica Studio, London, England.
**'Rockestra Theme' (McCartney)**
Paul McCartney (piano, keyboards), Denny Laine (guitar), Laurence Juber (guitar), Dave Gilmour (guitar), Hank Marvin (guitar), Pete Townshend (guitar), Steve Holly (drums), John Bonham (drums), Kenny Jones (drums), John Paul Jones (bass, piano), Ronnie Lane (bass), Bruce Thomas (bass), Gary Brooker (piano), John Paul Jones (piano), Linda McCartney (keyboards), Tony Ashton (keyboards), Speedy Acquaye, Tony Carr, Ray Cooper, Morris Pert (percussion), Howie Casey (saxophone), Tony Dorsey (trombone), Steve Howard (trumpet), Thaddeus Richard (saxophone). Recorded at Abbey Road Studios, London, England.
**'To You' (McCartney)**
Paul McCartney (bass, keyboards, vocals), Linda McCartney (keyboards, backing vocals), Denny Laine (guitar, backing vocals), Laurence Juber (guitar), Steve Holly (drums). Recorded at Spirit Of Ranachan Studio.
**'After The Ball' (McCartney)**
Paul McCartney (piano, vocals) Linda McCartney (keyboards, backing vocals), Denny Laine (guitar, backing vocals), Laurence Juber (guitar), Steve Holly (drums). Mobile Studio recording at Lympne Castle.
**'Million Miles' (McCartney)**
Paul McCartney (concertina, vocals). Mobile Studio recording at Lympne Castle.
**'Winter Rose' (McCartney)**
Paul McCartney (piano, harpsichord, bass, vocals), Linda McCartney (backing vocals), Denny Laine (guitar, backing vocals), Laurence Juber (guitar), Steve Holly (drums). Recorded at Spirit Of Ranachan Studio.

**'Love Awake' (McCartney)**
Paul McCartney (guitar, vocals), Linda McCartney (organ, backing vocals), Denny Laine (guitar, backing vocals), Laurence Juber (guitar), Steve Holly (drums), The Black Dyke Mills Band (horns). Mobile Studio recording at Lympne Castle, and at Abbey Road.

**'The Broadcast' (McCartney)**
Paul McCartney (piano), Mr Margary (recitation). Mobile Studio recording at Lympne Castle.

**'So Glad To See You Here' (McCartney)**
Personnel as 'Rockestra Theme'. Recorded at Abbey Road.

**'Baby's Request' (McCartney)**
Paul McCartney (bass, piano, vocals), Linda McCartney (keyboards, backing vocals), Denny Laine (guitar), Laurence Juber (guitar), Steve Holly (drums). Recorded at Abbey Road.

All produced by Paul McCartney and Chris Thomas.


BACK TO THE EGG
Wings' seventh studio album was the first by the Mk.7 line-up (Paul, Linda, and Denny Laine, with the addition of Laurence Juber and Steve Holly). It would also turn out to be the last Wings album. With the departure of McCulloch and English in the summer of 1977, the group had again returned to its core line-up of McCartney–Laine–McCartney. Once London Town was completed, McCartney wasted no time recruiting replacements, both of whom came via recommendations from Denny Laine.

Laine met Steve Holly when he moved to the drummer's home village and employed him to play on a solo album he was recording. McCartney heard Holly's drumming when Laine played him some of the finished songs and invited him to audition in the basement of his London office. The drummer didn't have to wait long to discover if he had the job. "We played for about two or three hours," Holly recalled, "and Paul suddenly said, 'Fine. That's a good group: sounds great, let's go for it.'" McCartney said that after Joe English left he wanted "a really good drummer who was kinda heavy. We wanted an English sort of drummer." Holly was both heavy and English and impressed McCartney. "Steve's very good, no messing about and he can play anything. He's a good stable character, too, you can lean on him a bit." Holly's first job with Wings was filming the promotional video for 'With A Little Luck' on March 21 1978.

Laurence Juber was a session guitarist who'd previously appeared with Laine on The David Essex Show and had so impressed him with his playing that he got the job as Wings' lead guitarist. Growing tired of session work, Juber joined Wings because "I needed to get back to a basic rock thing, to learn the discipline of doing that... I needed to get away from the technical aspects of playing and get more into the guts of it." Joining the band about two months after Holly, Juber was installed as second guitarist in time to appear in the video for 'I've Had Enough'.

With the new line-up assembled, rehearsals and recording sessions were arranged for the next Wings album. As Linda had just given birth to the McCartneys' first son, exotic recording locations were abandoned in favour of more modest surroundings nearer to home. Sessions began on the McCartneys' Scottish farm at the makeshift Spirit Of Ranachan studio on June 29 1978 and lasted for five weeks, until July 27. This remote location gave the album the working title *Wings In The Wild*, later dropped in favour of *We're Open Tonight*, before McCartney finally settled on *Back To The Egg*.

After a summer break, sessions resumed at Lympne (pronounced Lim) castle in Kent, from September 11–29 1978. Wings then moved to Abbey Road and the recently constructed Replica Studio to complete the album. The stereo master was finished on April 1 1979.

Speaking to the *NME* about *London Town*, McCartney had hinted that he wanted a tougher rock sound for the next album. "We didn't seem to be writing any real hard rockers," he explained. "Next time round well go for a bit more sweat." *Back To The Egg* was a lot more sweaty than its predecessor and found McCartney ditching some of the lighter pop sensibilities that had dogged him in the past. Wings' tougher sonic signature mirrored what was happening at the time. "The new wave thing was just happening," McCartney recalled, "and I just realised that a lot of new wave was ... taking things at a faster tempo than we do. 'We' being what I call the Permanent Wave."

By far the most sonically dense album Wings recorded, *Back To The Egg* was an album of rock'n'roll chiaroscuro in which the dark rockers are perfectly balanced by the brighter ballads. This time McCartney didn't compromise, and that gives it an edge. If McCartney was trying to compete with the new wave upstarts he did a pretty good job, but compared with even the popier new wave bands, Wings lacked the amphetamine rush that defined the new wave. As anybody who saw Wings on their last British tour will testify, McCartney was a pop showman through and through, and *Back To The Egg* was little more than a sonic diversion than serious attempt to show the new wave that the old wave still had a fire in its belly and a gram of speed in its pocket.

As Wings were not planning to tour until the end of the year, and then only in Britain, McCartney commissioned Keff and Co to produce seven videos to promote the album. Filmed in and around Lympne Castle, they were designed to be shown individually or as a half-hour film (which was how they appeared when screened by the BBC). McCartney said that another major film project was in pre-production. MPL commissioned Willy Russell, author of the stage play *John, Paul, George, Ringo And Bert*, to write a film script for Wings. The film was tentatively titled *Band On The Run* and would have featured plenty of live footage as well as some form of narrative, but it never got past the planning stages.

As with previous albums, there were a number of outtakes. Superfluous songs by Laine and Juber eventually surfaced on solo albums, but most of McCartney's outtakes remain locked in the archives. While at Lympne, he wrote and recorded 'Robbers Ball', allegedly in one day, and completed another song, 'Cage'. Wings recorded an instrumental, 'Ranachan Rock', but this too failed to make the album.

Many albums generate outtakes, but few recording projects generate a complete album of unreleased songs. That is, however, what happened with *Back To The Egg*. While recording at Spirit Of Ranachan, Wings recorded 12 songs in one day for a proposed Rupert The Bear film soundtrack. (They were 'Rupert Song 1', 'Tippi Tippi Toes', 'Flying Horses', 'When The Wind Is Blowing', 'The Castle Of The King Of The Birds', 'Sunshine Sometime', 'Sea – Cornish Water', 'Storm', 'Nutwood Scene',

'Walking In The Meadow', 'Sea Melody', and 'Rupert Song 2'. 'Sunshine Sometime' and 'When The Wind Is Blowing' both date from late 1970. 'Sea Melody' was later adapted for *Standing Stone*. These demo recordings were scrapped when McCartney abandoned the idea of a feature-length film and began work on the less ambitious *Rupert And The Frog Song* animated short.)

After completing *Back To The Egg*, Wings took a summer break before returning to work in the autumn. Rehearsals were held for a short British tour, which took place during November and December 1979. The band were booked into small theatres rather than large stadiums – the largest date on the tour was the 10,000 capacity Wembley Arena. McCartney explained that he chose to play smaller venues to create a "feeling of togetherness as a group that you get from playing in front of an audience". The final night of the tour was officially Glasgow on December 17, but Wings made their last live appearance at the Hammersmith Odeon on December 29.

UN Secretary General Waldheim approached McCartney and asked if Wings could give a charity concert for the war-ravaged people of Kampuchea (Cambodia). This developed into a series of concerts at the Hammersmith Odeon that featured The Who, Queen, and The Clash as headliners. A great deal of speculation surrounded what turned out to be Wings' final concert: rumours circulated that McCartney might just be joined by the other ex-Beatles, but needless to say the proposed reunion didn't happen. However, McCartney surprised the audience by performing an encore with most of the Rockestra line-up, which was augmented with several performers who'd supported Wings earlier that evening.

Although history would record this as Wings' final live appearance, the band was far from finished. A concert tour of Japan was planned for January 1980, as well as proposed dates in China. However, a certain incident in Japan upset Wings' touring plans, and the band remained dormant during most of 1980. In October of that year, the group recorded more overdubs for McCartney's long-standing *Cold Cuts* album and commenced rehearsals for a proposed European tour and their next album, *Tug Of War*. (McCarteny began compiling *Hot Hits And Kold Kuts*, as it was originally titled, in the mid 1970s. Originally planned as a two-record set – hits on one disc, outtakes on the other – it was shelved in the early 1980s. Several songs intended for the *Cold Cuts* album were later issued as B-sides.)

### Back To The Egg songs
'Reception' is the first of two short instrumentals recorded during Wings' residency at Lympne Castle. An early version of 2:32 duration had the main motif from *The Broadcast* superimposed over Wings' funky backing. Although McCartney probably intended to create a sense of incongruity, the result was ultimately messy and ditched.

Edited considerably for the album, 'Reception' remains little more than a doodle. McCartney's bass riff establishes a groove over which he places a random radio-scan and recitation by Mrs Margary (the early version had featured additional spoken passages from both Mr and Mrs Margary, owners of Lympne Castle). The use of a radio as a chance generating mechanism was used by John Cage for his musique concrète experiments and appropriated by The Beatles for Lennon's 'I Am The Walrus', but here it's employed more for effect than for intellectual reasons. "We wanted it to be submerged in this radio reception thing," explained McCartney, "so we made up a classical orchestra of our own with mellotrons and gizmos, and that's the background to the track."

McCartney had microphones set up on a spiral staircase at Lympne Castle for the recording of 'We're Open Tonight'. It's a simple ballad with a fragile acoustic guitar motif, and at one point its title was considered as a possible album title, but as with other ideas it was rejected.

Like many of the songs recorded at Spirit Of Ranachan, Laine's 'Again And Again And Again' was cut live, with guitar overdubs added later. Originally Laine had two separate songs, 'Little Woman' and 'Again And Again And Again' but combined them at McCartney's suggestion. It's a competent but uninspired Laine composition, and one of the weaker songs on the album.

'Arrow Through Me' finds McCartney bemoaning the pain of rejection and, uncharacteristically, casting himself as the loser. Even if his pessimistic lyric was autobiographical, his disappointment was masked by a buoyant melody. If this is a confession – and there's little to indicate a declaration of guilt and no attempt to match melody with narrative – then it's one scored through with ambivalence.
A solo recording by McCartney with Holly on drums, the basic track was recorded in Scotland, completed with overdubs at Replica Studios, London, in October 1978. At one point, it was given a saxophone solo, but this was deleted from the released version.

For 'Rockestra Theme', recorded at Abbey Road on October 3 1978, McCartney assembled some of Britain's finest musicians. Although almost everyone who'd been invited turned up, several of his musician friends failed to appear. Sadly, Keith Moon died the week before the session took place. Eric Clapton was invited but didn't arrive because, McCartney explained, "he didn't feel like it". Jeff Beck failed to show because he wanted to veto the track if he didn't like the way it turned out. Jimmy Page was also invited to the session, but he too failed to turn up. Laurence Juber recalled: "Jimmy Page never showed up. His amplifier was there but he never came. John Paul Jones is on the record and John Bonham. No Jimmy Page." However, it was Clapton, Beck and Page's loss, and McCartney took the view that whoever showed up would be the Rockestra. The only musician to play on the session who wasn't part of the rock establishment was Bruce Thomas, bassist with Elvis Costello & The Attractions. McCartney admired the group: he invited them to support Wings at the Hammersmith Odeon in December 1979 and eventually co-wrote several songs with their vocalist and songwriter, Elvis Costello.

Before recording began, McCartney played the assembled musicians a demo of 'Rockestra Theme', recorded by Wings at Lympne Castle. He then spent about an hour rehearsing the group before tapes rolled at around 2 o'clock. When recording did begin, everything came together remarkably quickly. "It's amazing how tightly they all played together," McCartney said. "With people like Pete Townshend, Gary Brooker, Hank Marvin, Ronnie Lane, Ray Cooper, and Dave Gilmour, you would have expected a rougher, less controlled sound. But it didn't turn out that way. When you get 14 rock musicians together for the first time, they can be incredibly tight."

The secret to its success was its simplicity. An over-elaborate arrangement would have detracted from the sheer power of the assembled group, whose sole purpose was to act as a whole rather than soloists. 'Rockestra Theme' was written as an ensemble piece, not to indulge the egos of those invited to take part. And this unity was reflected in the speed with which the ad-hoc group recorded the track. Only five takes were required before McCartney was satisfied that he had the track in the bag.

The event was filmed, which added to the technical problems involved in recording so many musicians at one time. In addition to a film crew and all of their equipment, which was hidden behind specially constructed false walls, the recording used 64 microphones and two synchronised tape recorders. McCartney got the Rockestra line-up to make one live appearance, too, which was also filmed and recorded as part of the Concerts For Kampuchea. (McCartney also produced a version of 'Rockestra Theme' for Duane Eddy's 1987 comeback album.)

With band, equipment, and the RAK mobile studio installed on McCartney's Scottish farm, recording commenced with an abrasive mid-tempo rocker, 'To You'. It was perhaps no surprise that McCartney, always perceptive to change, should react to current musical trends and produce a harsher, denser sound. When interviewed by Paul Gambaccini for *Rolling Stone* in 1979, he admitted to liking Supertramp's 'Logical Song' and Stevie Wonder, but also to liking "a few of the young bands ... I like Squeeze, Jam, and a few people. ... I like some of Elvis Costello's stuff. I like a lot of that stuff, anyway – the newer stuff."

The more musical of Britain's new wave groups shared with McCartney a common approach to melody, albeit one aligned with a rambunctious attitude to performance. While it's not surprising that he liked Squeeze or Costello, both of whom knew a good melody when they heard one, his admitting to liking Peter & The Test Tube Babies' 'Lord Lucan Is Missing' is more surprising. The corrosive bile that these bands spat into a jaded British music industry inevitably left its mark and affected McCartney's approach to *Back To The Egg*. Recording 'To You' was a simple enough affair: the basic backing track was laid down on the first day's recording; vocal harmonies and Juber's guitar solo were overdubbed the following day.

'After The Ball' is downbeat and tentative, and finds McCartney contemplating the unknown and searching for security in the familiar – which means Linda. Firmly rooted in apprehension, its funereal cadence and sober melody offer little hope of redemption, particularly as the song remains unresolved; it segues with the equally thoughtful 'Million Miles'. Nevertheless, there is some light at the end of the tunnel – but is this an elegy for a loss of self-belief, or a paean to hope?

McCartney began 'Million Miles' in 1974 but was unable to complete it satisfactorily. To solve the problem, he segued it with 'After The Ball', another incomplete song. It's essentially a solo track, and for the recording McCartney had a microphone set up on the roof of Lympne Castle and accompanied himself with some rudimentary concertina. 'Million Miles' consists of simple chords and a plaintive lyric; it hints at anticipation and attempts to conclude the questions raised in 'After The Ball', but McCartney's enquires into the human condition are eternal and as such unanswerable.

'Winter Rose' was written in late 1976 or early 1977, and McCartney recorded a solo demo prior to completing *London Town*. Wings then recorded the song, complete with an extended introduction, at Spirit of Ranachan, with McCartney on piano and harpsichord, and Laine and Juber on acoustic guitars. Its acoustic setting and sensitive arrangement evokes a dark, claustrophobic atmosphere that is contrasted with the optimistic lyric. The rose has often been employed as a metaphor for beauty and femininity; here it could symbolise Linda and the enchantment McCartney found in her radiant personality.

Wings recorded a version of 'Love Awake' during sessions at Spirit Of Ranachan in July 1979. Described by Mark Vigars – the album's engineer – as a "rough guide version", it was little more than a rambling demo. Featuring a distinct harmonica part, this demo recording lasted 6:30. Re-recorded while Wings were encamped at Lympne Castle, the song's arrangement originally featured a slide guitar part, but this was scrapped when The Black Dyke Mills Band overdubbed a brass part at Abbey Road. Once the brass was in place, McCartney replaced his guide vocal to complete the recording.

'The Broadcast' was originally a brief acoustic-guitar instrumental, which McCartney recorded in 1977. Recorded at Lympne Castle by Wings, with McCartney on piano, it featured a vocal contribution from the castle's owner, Mr Margary. McCartney coaxed Mr Margary into reciting extracts from works by John Galsworthy and Ian Hay, while his wife appears on 'Reception', briefly reciting an extract from *The Poodle and the Pug* by A. P. Herbert. "The fellow who owns the castle has got a very BBC voice," recalled McCartney, "so we were sitting around one evening and I asked him, just for a laugh, if he would do the talking bit, and he said he'd be pleased to. We got him in the old kitchen, and we got a big fire crackling, and sat down and just read out a couple of books he had in the library. Well we liked his bit so much… it's got pathos to it… everyone felt when they heard it that they should stand up and salute."

'So Glad To See You Here' was recorded about an hour after completing 'Rockestra Theme'. Again, the backing track was recorded live, with McCartney supplying a rough guide vocal, which he replaced the following day. At the same overdub session, Linda and Laine added their harmonies. The reggae-influenced coda, which incorporates the opening line from 'We're Open Tonight', was added later by Wings.

McCartney wrote 'Baby's Request' in France, and it was originally intended as a demo for the old vocal group The Mills Brothers. At first, McCartney thought the song corny, but he was swayed into recording it by his children. Considering that Wings had recorded the 'Rockestra Theme' the previous week, if nothing else 'Baby's Request' was a testament to the band's versatility. McCartney delivers a convincing vocal and Juber, who had been a member of the National Youth Jazz Orchestra, supplies some authentic jazz phrasing that captures a certain period feel. Although the song had not been intended for *Back To The Egg,* it replaced 'Cage', recorded at Lympne and originally destined for the album.

### Back To The Egg data

Parlophone issued *Back To The Egg* with customised 'egg' labels and picture inner sleeve. Publicity and promotion generated two very collectable items. A boxed-set was produced containing a copy of the album, a set of tea cards, an egg-shaped badge, key-ring, promotional photographs, and a T-shirt. EMI also pressed 100 copies of a picture-disc version of the album (PCTCP 257) that featured the front cover artwork on both sides. This was issued in the commercial album sleeve but with a large circular hole die cut into the front cover to reveal the picture disc. Other items, such as an egg-shaped jigsaw puzzle and lavish in-store displays, were employed to promote the album.

In the USA, Columbia issued the album (FC 36057) with artwork and customised labels identical to the British edition. It also issued the album on 8-track (FCA 36057).

The CD was issued a full 10 years after the album first appeared. When McCartney re-signed with Capitol the company issued *Back To The Egg* on CD (48200) in 1989. The album was issued on CD (CDP 7 89136) in Britain with bonus tracks in 1993.

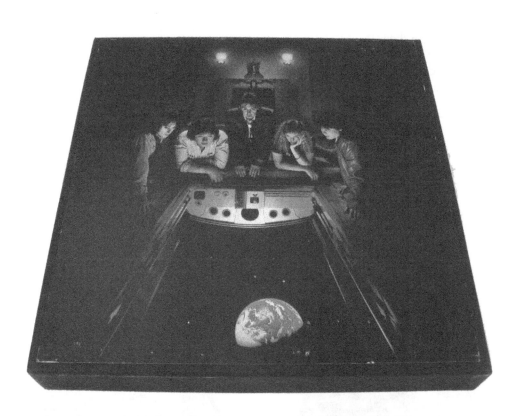

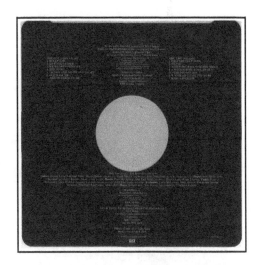

## 'GETTING CLOSER' / 'BABY'S REQUEST'
## WINGS
**UK release** August 10 1979; Parlophone 6027; chart high No.60.

### 'GETTING CLOSER'
Parlophone issued Wings' final British single, 'Getting Closer' / 'Baby's Request', with customised 'egg' labels in a picture sleeve, bought off-the-shelf from Hipgnosis. Demo copies are identical to the commercial release except they have 'DEMO RECORD NOT FOR SALE' in black text printed above the spindle hole.

## ARROW THROUGH ME' / 'OLD SIAM, SIR'
## WINGS
**US release** August 13 1979; Columbia 3-11070; chart high No. 29.

### 'ARROW THROUGH ME'
Columbia issued 'Arrow Through Me' / 'Old Siam, Sir' as Wings' final US single. It was issued with generic Columbia labels and paper sleeve. A Top 30 hit in America, it did even better in Canada where it peaked at Number 6. Demonstration copies of the A-side were issued with white labels with black text and the large red Columbia logo at top centre of the label. The single was issued in Japan by Odeon (EPR-20657).

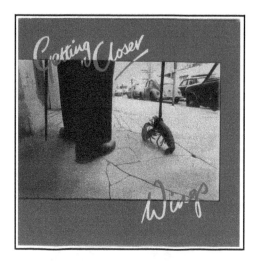

Australian issue

Spanish issue

## 'WONDERFUL CHRISTMASTIME' / 'RUDOLPH THE RED-NOSED REGGAE'
## PAUL McCARTNEY
**UK release** November 16 1979; Parlophone R 6029; chart high No.6.
**US release** November 26 1979; Columbia 3-11162; chart high No.8.

### 'Wonderful Christmastime' (McCartney)
Paul McCartney (bass, guitar, keyboards, drums, percussion, vocals). Recorded at home studio, Peasmarsh, Sussex or The Barn, High Park Farm, Scotland.
### 'Rudolph The Red-Nosed Reggae' (Marks)
Paul McCartney (harpsichord, drums) Bob Loveday (violin). Recorded at Abbey Road Studios, London, England.
Both produced by Paul McCartney.

'WONDERFUL CHRISTMASTIME'
McCartney's attempt at a Christmas hit was, like most Christmas singles, recorded in the summer. It was made while he worked on *McCartney II* and became his first solo single since 'The Back Seat Of My Car', marking the beginning of the end for Wings.

'Wonderful Christmastime' is the kind of ditty McCartney had previously knocked out for The Beatles' latter Christmas records. Although it has more substance that 'Everywhere It's Christmas' or 'Happy Christmas, Happy New Year' it has limited appeal, even in the season of goodwill. Despite this, it did rather well and sold better than any of the singles taken from *Back To The Egg*. Released to coincide with Wings' British tour, which no doubt helped – it was performed nightly in front of packed houses – the single made its way deep into the Top 10. It was equally as successful on the other side of the Atlantic where it also went top ten. 'Wonderful Christmastime' became something of a favourite with compilers of Christmas albums, in particular EMI's perennial *Now That's What I Call Christmas*, on which it appeared a number of times.

The solo instrumental reading of 'Rudolph The Red-Nosed Reindeer' was recorded in 1975 and dusted off for this B-side. Bob Loveday, who just happened to be delivering a violin to the studio, also plays. Even with a subtle change to the title, the arrangement is as far from reggae as you can get. This remains, perhaps, the nadir of McCartney's career.

### 'Wonderful Christmastime' data
Parlophone issued the single with generic labels and picture sleeve. Demonstration copies replicate the commercial pressing but with a large 'A' at 10 o'clock and 'DEMO NOT FOR SALE' on three lines above the spindle hole.

The Columbia issue came with generic labels, and picture sleeve identical to the British release. Columbia issued demonstration copies of the A-side with white labels with black text and the large Columbia logo in red, at top centre of the label. In 1983, Columbia reissued the single (38-040127) with a 'UPC' logo printed on the label and a stereo B-side (original pressings have the B-side in mono). In 1994, Capitol Records re-released the single on red vinyl (S7-17643-A).

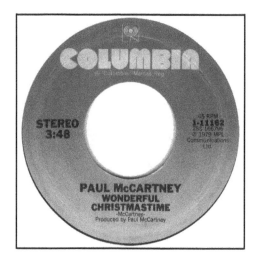

# Discography

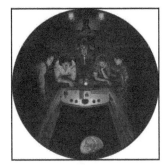

## UK LPs

| | | |
|---|---|---|
| 06.01.67 | The Family Way | Decca LK 4847/SKL 4847 |
| 17.04.70 | McCartney | Apple PCS 7102 |
| 21.05.71 | Ram | Apple PAS 10003 |
| 15.11.71 | Wild Life | Apple PCS 7142 |
| 03.05.73 | Red Rose Speedway | Apple PCTC 251 |
| 06.07.73 | Live And Let Die O.S.T. | United Artists UAS 29475 |
| 30.11.73 | Band On The Run | Apple PAS 10007 |
| 30.05.75 | Venus And Mars | Capitol PCTC 254 |
| 26.03.76 | Wings At The Speed Of Sound | Capitol PAS 10010 |
| 10.12.76 | Wings Over America | Capitol PCSP 720 |
| 29.04.77 | Thrillington | Regal Zonophone EMC 2954 |
| 31.03.78 | London Town | Parlophone PAS 10012 |
| 01.12.78 | Wings Greatest | Parlophone PCTC 256 |
| 08.06.79 | Back To The Egg | Parlophone PCTC 257 |

## UK 8-TRACK CARTRIDGES

| | | |
|---|---|---|
| 17.04.70 | McCartney | Apple 8X-PCS 7102 |
| 21.05.71 | Ram | Apple 8X-PAS 10003 |
| 15.11.71 | Wild Life | Apple 8X-PCS 7142 |
| 03.05.73 | Red Rose Speedway | Apple 8X-PCTC 251 |
| 00.01.74 | Band On The Run | Apple 8X-PAS 10007 |
| 30.05.75 | Venus And Mars | Parlophone 8X-PCTC 2541 |
| 26.03.76 | Wings At The Speed Of Sound | Parlophone 8X-PAS 10010 |
| 10.12.76 | Wings Over America | Parlophone 8X-PCSP 720 |

## UK REEL-TO-REEL TAPES

| | | |
|---|---|---|
| 17.04.70 | McCartney | Apple TA-PMC 7102 |

## UK 7-INCH SINGLES

| | | |
|---|---|---|
| 19.02.71 | 'Another Day' / 'Oh Woman Oh Why' | Apple R 5889 |
| 13.08.71 | 'The Back Seat Of My Car' / 'Heart Of The Country' | Apple R 5914 |
| 25.02.72 | 'Give Ireland Back To The Irish' / 'Give Ireland Back To The Irish' (Version) | Apple R 5963 |
| 05.05.72 | 'Mary Had A Little Lamb' / 'Little Woman Love' | Apple R 5949 |
| 01.12.72 | 'Hi, Hi, Hi' / 'C Moon' | Apple R 5973 |
| 23.03.73 | 'My Love' / 'The Mess' | Apple R 5985 |
| 01.06.73 | 'Live And Let Die' / 'I Lie Around' | Apple R 5987 |
| 26.10.73 | 'Helen Wheels' / 'Country Dreamer' | Apple R 5993 |
| 18.02.74 | 'Jet' / 'Let Me Roll It' | Apple R 5996 |
| 28.06.74 | 'Band On The Run' / 'Zoo Gang' | Apple R 5997 |
| 18.10.74 | 'Walking In The Park With Eloise' / 'Bridge Over The River Suite' | EMI 2220 |
| 25.10.74 | 'Junior's Farm' / 'Sally G' | Apple R 5999 |
| 07.02.75 | 'Sally G' / 'Junior's Farm' | Apple R 5999 |
| 16.05.75 | 'Listen To What The Man Said' / 'Love In Song' | Capitol R 6006 |
| 05.09.75 | 'Letting Go' / 'You Gave Me The Answer' | Capitol R 6008 |
| 28.11.75 | 'Venus And Mars' / 'Rock Show', 'Magneto And Titanium Man' | Capitol R 6010 |
| 00.00.76 | 'Another Day' / 'Oh Woman Oh Why' | Capitol R 5889 |
| 00.00.76 | 'The Back Seat Of My Car' / 'Heart Of The Country' | Capitol R 5914 |
| 00.00.76 | 'Give Ireland Back To The Irish' / 'Give Ireland Back To The Irish' (Version) | Capitol R 5963 |
| 00.00.76 | 'Mary Had A Little Lamb' / 'Little Woman Love' | Capitol R 5949 |
| 00.00.76 | 'Hi, Hi, Hi' / 'C Moon' | Capitol R 5973 |
| 00.00.76 | 'My Love' / 'The Mess' | Capitol R 5985 |
| 00.00.76 | 'Live And Let Die' / 'I Lie Around' | Capitol R 5987 |
| 00.00.76 | 'Helen Wheels' / 'Country Dreamer' | Capitol R 5993 |
| 00.00.76 | 'Jet' / 'Let Me Roll It' | Capitol R 5996 |
| 00.00.76 | 'Band On The Run' / 'Zoo Gang' | Capitol R 5997 |
| 30.04.76 | 'Silly Love Songs' / 'Cook Of The House' | Parlophone R 6014 |
| 23.07.76 | 'Let 'Em In' / 'Beware My Love' | Parlophone R 6015 |

04.02.77 'Maybe I'm Amazed' / 'Soily'                    Parlophone R 60
00.04.77 'Uncle Albert/Admiral Halsey' / 'Eat At Home'  Regal Zonophone 2594
11.11.77 'Mull Of Kintyre' / 'Girls' School'            Parlophone R 6018
23.03.78 'With A Little Luck' / 'Backwards Traveller/Cuff Link'  Parlophone R 6019
16.06.78 'I've Had Enough' / 'Deliver Your Children'    Parlophone R 6020
11.08.78 'London Town' / 'I'm Carrying'                  Parlophone R 6021
23.03.79 'Goodnight Tonight' / 'Daytime Nightime Suffering'  Parlophone R 6023
01.06.79 'Old Siam Sir' / 'Spin It On'                   Parlophone R 6026
10.08.79 'Getting Closer' / 'Baby's Request'             Parlophone R 6027
10.08.79 'Seaside Woman' / 'B Side To Seaside'           A&M AMS 7461
16.11.79 'Wonderful Christmastime' / 'Rudolph The Red-Nosed Reggae'  Parlophone R 6029

## UK 12-INCH SINGLES
23.03.79 'Goodnight Tonight' (Extended) / 'Daytime Nightime Suffering'  Parlophone 12Y R 6023
10.08.79 'Seaside Woman' / 'B Side To Seaside'           A&M AMSP 7461

## UK 7-INCH SINGLE PROMOS

28.06.74 'Band On The Run' (Edit) / 'Band On The Run' white label, black text Apple R 5997
28.06.74 'Band On The Run' / 'Let Me Roll It' white label, black text with 'FROM THE ALBUM "BAND ON THE RUN" PAS10007' on three lines top centre        Apple PSR 359
25.10.74 'Junior's Farm' (Edit) / 'Sally G'              Apple R 5999
07.02.75 'Sally G' / 'Junior's Farm'                     Apple R 5999
30.04.76 'Silly Love Songs' (Edit) / 'Silly Love Songs'  Parlophone R 6014
23.07.76 'Let 'Em In' (Edit) / 'Beware My Love'          Parlophone R 6015
11.11.77 'Mull Of Kintyre' (Edit) / 'Girls' School' (Edit)  Parlophone R 6018
23.03.78 'With A Little Luck' (Edit) / 'Backwards Traveller/Cuff Link'  Parlophone R 6019

## US LPs
24.04.67 *The Family Way*                 London M 76007/MS 82007
20.04.70 *McCartney*                       Apple STAO-3363
17.05.71 *Ram (mono promo in stereo cover)*  Apple MAS-3375
17.05.71 *Ram*                             Apple SMAS-3375
06.12.71 *Wild Life*                        Apple SW 3386
30.04.73 *Red Rose Speedway*               Apple SMAL-3409
03.12.73 *Band On The Run*                 Apple SO-3415
27.05.75 *Venus And Mars*                   Capitol SMAS-11419
22.03.76 *Wings At The Speed Of Sound*      Capitol SW-11525
10.12.76 *Wings Over America*               Capitol SWCO-11593
10.12.76 *McCartney*                        Capitol SMAS-3363
00.00.76 *Ram*                              Capitol SMAS-3375
00.00.76 *Wild Life*                        Capitol SW-3386
00.00.76 *Red Rose Speedway*                Capitol SMAL-3409
00.00.76 *Band On The Run*                  Capitol SO-3415
16.05.77 *Thrillington*                     Capitol ST-11642
27.03.78 *London Town*                      Capitol SW-11777
27.11.78 *Wings Greatest*                   Capitol SOO-11905
00.12.78 *Band On The Run (Picture Disc)*   Capitol SEAX 11901
11.06.79 *Back To The Egg* *                Columbia FC- 36057

## US 8-TRACK CARTRIDGES
*McCartney*                                Apple 8XT 3363
*Wild Life*                                Apple 8XW 3386
*Red Rose Speedway*                        Apple 8XW 3409
*Band On The Run*                          Apple 8XZ 3415
*Band On The Run (Quadraphonic Mix)*       Apple Q8W 3415
*Venus And Mars*                           Capitol 8XT 11419
*Venus And Mars (Quadraphonic Mix)*        Capitol Q8W 11419
*Wings At The Speed Of Sound*              Capitol 8XW 11525

| | |
|---|---|
| *Wings Over America* | Capitol 8X3C-11593 |
| *Thrillington* | Capitol 8XT 11642 |
| *London Town* | Capitol 8XW 11777 |
| *Wings Greatest* | Capitol 8XOO 11905 |
| *Live And Let Die* | United Artists EA-100 |
| *Back To The Egg* | Columbia FCA 36057 |

## US REEL-TO-REEL TAPES

| | |
|---|---|
| *The Family Way* | London/Ampex LPL-70136 |
| *McCartney* | Apple/Ampex L-3363 |
| *Ram* | Apple/Ampex 3375 |
| *Live And Let Die* | United Artists UST-100A |

## US 7-INCH SINGLES

22.02.71 'Another Day' / 'Oh Woman Oh Why'      Apple 1829
02.08.71 'Uncle Albert/Admiral Halsey' / 'Too Many People' Apple 1837
28.02.72 'Give Ireland Back To The Irish' / 'Give Ireland Back To The Irish' (Version) Apple 1847
29.05.72 'Mary Had A Little Lamb' / 'Little Woman Love' Apple 1851
04.12.72 'Hi, Hi, Hi' / 'C Moon'      Apple 1857
09.04.73 'My Love' / 'The Mess'      Apple 1861
18.06.73 'Live And Let Die' / 'I Lie Around'      Apple 1863
12.11.73 'Helen Wheels' / 'Country Dreamer'      Apple 1869
28.01.74 'Jet' / 'Mamunia'      Apple 1871
18.02.74 'Jet' / 'Let Me Roll It'      Apple 1871
08.04.74 'Band On The Run' / 'Nineteen Hundred And Eighty Five' Apple 1873
02.12.74 'Walking In The Park With Eloise' / 'Bridge Over The River Suite' EMI 3977
04.11.74 'Junior's Farm' / 'Sally G'      Apple 1875
24.12.74 'Sally G' / 'Junior's Farm'      Apple 1875
26.05.75 'Listen To What The Man Said' / 'Love In Song' Capitol 4091
29.09.75 'Letting Go' / 'You Gave Me The Answer'   Capitol 4145
27.10.75 'Venus And Mars/Rock Show', 'Magneto And Titanium Man' Capitol 4175
01.04.76 'Silly Love Songs' / 'Cook Of The House'      Capitol 4256
01.04.76 'Silly Love Songs'/ 'Cook Of The House' black label Capitol 4256
28.06.76 'Let 'Em I'n / 'Beware My Love'      Capitol 4293
28.06.76 'Let 'Em I'n / 'Beware My Love' black label  Capitol 4293
00.00.76 'Another Day' / 'Oh Woman Oh Why?' black label Capitol 1829
00.00.76 'Uncle Albert/Admiral Halsey' / 'To Many People' black label Capitol 1837
00.00.76 'Give Ireland Back To The Irish' / 'Give Ireland Back To The Irish' (Version)
                               black label Capitol 1847
00.00.76 'Mary Had A Little Lamb' / 'Little Woman Love' black label Capitol 1851
00.00.76 'Hi, Hi, Hi' / 'C Moon' black label      Capitol 1857
00.00.76 'My Love' / 'The Mess' black label      Capitol 1861
00.00.76 'Live And Let Die' / 'I Lie Around' black label Capitol 1863
00.00.76 'Helen Wheels' / 'Country Dreamer' black label Capitol 1869
00.00.76 'Jet' / 'Let Me Roll It' black label      Capitol 1871
00.00.76 'Band On The Run' / 'Nineteen Hundred And Eighty Five' black label Capitol 1873
07.02.77 'Maybe I'm Amazed' / 'Soily'      Capitol 4385
07.02.77 'Maybe I'm Amazed' / 'Soily' black label   Capitol 4385
31.05.77 'Seaside Woman' / 'B Side To Seaside'   Epic 8-50403
14.11.77 'Mull Of Kintyre' / 'Girls' School'      Capitol 4504
00.00.78 'Mull Of Kintyre' / 'Girls' School' purple label Capitol 4504
20.03.78 'With A Little Luck' / 'Backwards Traveller/Cuff Link' Capitol 4559
05.06.78 I''ve Had Enough' / 'Deliver Your Children' Capitol 4594
14.08.78 'London Town' / 'I'm Carrying'      Capitol 4625
19.03.79 'Goodnight Tonight' / 'Daytime Nightime Suffering' Columbia 3-10939
04.06.79 'Getting Closer' / 'Spin It O'n      Columbia 3-11020
13.08.79 'Arrow Through Me' / 'Old Siam Sir'   Columbia 3-11070
26.11.79 'Wonderful Christmastime' / 'Rudolph The Red-Nosed Reggae' Columbia 3-11162

## US 7-INCH SINGLE PROMOS

| | |
|---|---|
| 'Another Day' mono | Apple PRO-6193 |
| 'Uncle Albert/Admiral Halsey' mono | Apple PRO-6278 |
| 'Hi, Hi, Hi' / 'C Moon' | Apple P-1857 |
| 'My Love' mono/stereo | Apple P-1861 |
| 'Live And Let Die' mono/stereo | Apple P-1863 |
| 'Helen Wheels' mono/stereo | Apple PRO-6786 |
| 'Country Dreamer' mono/stereo | Apple PRO-6787 |
| 'Jet' mono/stereo | Apple P-1871 |
| 'Jet' mono (Edit) | Apple PRO-6872 |
| 'Band On The Run' mono (Edit) /stereo | Apple PRO-6285 |
| 'Band On The Run' mono (Edit) /stereo (Edit) | Apple P-1873 |
| 'Junior's Farm' mono (Edit)/stereo | Apple P-1875 |
| 'Junior's Farm' (Edit) white label | Apple SPRO-8003 |
| 'Sally G 'mono/stereo | Apple P-1875 |
| 'Listen To What The Man Said' mono/stereo | Capitol P-4093 |
| 'Letting Go' mono/stereo | Capitol P4145 |
| 'Venus And Mars/Rock Show' mono/stereo | Capitol P-4175 |
| 'Let 'Em In' mono/stereo | Capitol P-4293 |
| 'Silly Love Songs' mono/stereo | Capitol P-4256 |
| 'Maybe I'm Amazed' mono/stereo | Capitol PRO-8570 |
| 'Seaside Woman' / 'B Side To Seaside' some red vinyl | Epic 8-50403 |
| With A Little Luck      (Edit) stereo | Capitol PRO-8812 |
| 'London Town' mono/stereo | Capitol P-4625 |
| 'I've Had Enough' | Capitol PRO-8860 |
| 'Mull Of Kintyre' (Edit) | Capitol SPRO-8746 |
| 'Goodnight Tonight' mono/stereo | Columbia 3-10939 |
| 'Getting Closer' mono/stereo | Columbia 3-11020 |
| 'Arrow Through Me' mono/stereo | Columbia 1-11070 |
| 'Wonderful Christmastime' mono/stereo | Columbia 1-11162 |

## US 12-INCH SINGLE PROMOS

| | |
|---|---|
| 'Brung To You By' | Apple SPRO-6210 |
| 'Maybe I'm Amazed' mono/stereo | Capitol PRO-8574 |
| 'Goodnight Tonight' long/short stereo | Columbia 23-10940 |

## JAPANESE LPs

| | |
|---|---|
| McCartney | Apple AP-80377 |
| McCartney | Odeon EPS-80231 |
| Ram | Apple AP-80283 |
| Ram | Odeon EPS-80232 |
| Wild Life | Apple AP-80283 |
| Wild Life | Odeon EPS-80233 |
| Red Rose Speedway | Apple EAP80813 |
| Red Rose Speedway | Odeon EPS 80234 |
| Band On The Run | Apple EAP-80951 |
| Band On The Run | Odeon EPS-80235 |
| Band On The Run picture disc, lyric insert | Odeon EPS-90073 |
| Venus And Mars | Capitol EAP-80813 |
| Venus And Mars | Odeon EPS-80236 |
| At The Speed Of Sound | Capitol EPS-80510 |
| Wings Over America | Capitol EPS-50001-3 |
| London Town | Capitol EPS-81000 |
| Wings Greatest | Odeon EPS-81150 |
| Back To The Egg | Odeon EPS-81200 |

# JAPANESE SINGLES

**Key** GS = gatefold sleeve; SS = single-sheet sleeve; TS = trifold sleeve; LSI = lyric sheet insert; PS = pocket sleeve;
4 = ¥400 on sleeve; 5 = ¥500 on sleeve; 6 = ¥600 on sleeve; 7 = ¥700 on sleeve.

| | |
|---|---|
| 'The Family Way' / 'Theme For Jenny' GS, ¥370 | London TOP-1177(S) |
| 'Another Day' / 'Oh Woman, Oh Why' GS, 4 or 5 | Apple AR-2771 |
| 'Another Day' / 'Oh Woman, Oh Why' GS, 5 | Capitol EPR-10780 |
| 'Another Day' / 'Oh Woman, Oh Why' GS, 7 | Odeon EPS-17191 |
| 'Eat At Home' / 'Smile Away' GS, 4 or 5 | Apple AR-2879 |
| 'Eat At Home' / 'Smile Away' GS, 5 | Capitol EPR-10781 |
| 'Eat At Home' / 'Smile Away' GS, 7 | Odeon EPS-17192 |
| 'Give Ireland Back To The Irish' / 'Give Ireland Back To The Irish' (Version) GS, 4 or 5 | Apple EAR-10013 |
| 'Give Ireland Back To The Irish' / 'Give Ireland Back To The Irish' (Version) GS, 5 | Capitol EPR-10782 |
| 'Give Ireland Back To The Irish' / 'Give Ireland Back To The Irish' (Version) GS, 7 | Odeon EPS-17193 |
| 'Mary Had A Little Lamb' / 'Little Woman Love' GS, 5 | Apple EAR-10083 |
| 'Mary Had A Little Lamb' / 'Little Woman Love' GS, 5 | Capitol EPR-10783 |
| 'Mary Had A Little Lamb' / 'Little Woman Love' GS, 7 | Odeon EPS-17194 |
| 'Hi Hi Hi' / 'C Moon' TS/GS, 5, red or black vinyl | Apple EAR-10241 |
| 'Hi Hi Hi' / 'C Moon' GS, 5 | Capitol EPR-10784 |
| 'Hi Hi Hi' / 'C Moon' GS, 7 | Odeon EPS-17195 |
| 'My Love' / 'The Mess' GS, 5 | Apple EAR-10350 |
| 'My Love' / 'The Mess' GS, 5 | Capitol EPR-10785 |
| 'My Love' / 'The Mess' GS, 7 | Odeon EPS-17196 |
| 'Live And Let Die' / 'I Lie Around' GS, 5 | Apple EAR-10401 |
| 'Live And Let Die' / 'I Lie Around' GS, 5 | Capitol EPR-10786 |
| 'Live And Let Die' / 'I Lie Around' GS, 7 | Odeon EPS-17197 |
| 'Helen Wheels' / 'Country Dreamer' GS, 5 | Apple EAR-10464 |
| 'Helen Wheels' / 'Country Dreamer' GS, 5 | Capitol EPR-10787 |
| 'Helen Wheels' / 'Country Dreamer' GS, 7 | Odeon EPS-17198 |
| 'Jet' / 'Let Me Roll It' GS, 5 | Apple EAR-10520 |
| 'Jet' / 'Let Me Roll It' SS, 5 | Capitol EPR-10788 |
| 'Jet '/ 'Let Me Roll It' SS, 7 | Odeon EPS-17199 |
| 'Band On The Run' / 'Nineteen Hundred And Eighty Five' GS, 5 | Apple EAR-10581 |
| 'Band On The Run' / 'Nineteen Hundred And Eighty Five' GS, 5 | Capitol EPR-10789 |
| 'Band On The Run' / 'Nineteen Hundred And Eighty Five' GS, 7 | Odeon EPS-17200 |
| 'Junior's Farm' / 'Sally G' GS, 5 | Apple EAR-10581 |
| 'Junior's Farm' / 'Sally G' SS, 5 | Capitol EPR-10790 |
| 'Junior's Farm' / 'Sally G' SS, 7 | Odeon EPS-17201 |
| 'Walking In The Park With Eloise' / 'Bridge Over The River Suite' Toshiba/EMI EMR-10706 | |
| 'Listen To What The Man Said' / 'Love In Song' PS, LSI, 5 | Capitol EPR-10777 |
| 'Listen To What The Man Said' / 'Love In Song' PS, LSI, 7 | Odeon EPS-17202 |
| 'Letting Go' / 'You Gave Me The Answer' SS, 5 | Capitol EPR-10863 |
| 'Letting Go' / 'You Gave Me The Answer' SS, 7 | Odeon EPS-17203 |
| 'Venus And Mars/Rock Show' / 'Magneto And Titanium Man' SS, 5 | Capitol EPR-10881 |
| 'Venus And Mars/Rock Show' / 'Magneto And Titanium Man' SS, 7 | Odeon EPS-17204 |
| 'Silly Love Songs' / 'Cook Of The House' SS, 6 | Capitol EPR-20020 |
| 'Silly Love Songs' / 'Cook Of The House' SS, 6 | Odeon EPR-20020 |
| 'Let 'Em In' / 'Beware My Love' SS, 6 | Capitol EPR-20070 |
| 'Let 'Em In' / 'Beware My Love' SS, 6 | Odeon EPR-20070 |
| 'Maybe I'm Amazed' / 'Soily' SS, 6 | Capitol EPR-20203 |
| 'Mull Of Kintyre' / 'Girl's School' PS, LSI, 6 | Capitol EPR-20370 |
| 'With A Little Luck' / 'Backwards Traveller/Cuff Link' SS, 6 | Capitol EPR-20430 |
| 'With A Little Luck' / 'Backwards Traveller/Cuff Link' promo (DJ USE ONLY) | Capitol PRP-1038. |
| 'I've Had Enough' / 'Deliver Your Children' SS, 6 | Capitol EPR-20470 |
| 'London Town' / 'I'm Carrying' SS, 6 | Capitol EPR-20502 |
| 'Goodnight Tonight' / 'Daytime Nightime Suffering' SS, 6 | Odeon EPR-20572 |
| 'Getting Closer' / 'Spin It On' SS, 6 | Odeon EPR-20600 |
| 'Wonderful Christmastime' / 'Rudolph The Red-Nosed Reggae' SS, 6 | Odeon EPR-20644 |
| 'Wonderful Christmastime' / 'Rudolph The Red-Nosed Reggae' SS, 7 | Odeon EPS-17291 |
| 'Arrow Through Me' / 'Old Siam Sir' SS, 6 | Odeon EPR-20572 |

# McCARTNEY COLLABORATIONS

Here we list Paul McCartney's contributions to the recorded work of other artists, as producer and/or musician.

**DONOVAN**
'Mellow Yellow' / 'Preachin' Love'
McCartney background vocals on A-side
Released January 1967
UK Pye 7N 17267
US Epic 10098

**MCGOUGH & MCGEAR**
*McGough & McGear*
McCartney co-produces with Andy Roberts, performs on some tracks
Released May 17 1968
UK Parlophone PMC/PCS 7047

**MARY HOPKIN**
'Those Were The Days' / 'Turn Turn Turn'
McCartney produces, performs
Released August 30 1968
UK Apple APPLE 2
US Apple 1801

**JACKIE LOMAX**
'Sour Milk Sea' / 'The Eagle Laughs At You'
McCartney performs on A-side
Released August 30 1968
UK Apple APPLE 3
US Apple 1802

**BLACK DYKE MILLS BAND**
'Thingumybob' / 'Yellow Submarine'
McCartney produces
Released September 6 1968
UK Apple APPLE 4
US Apple 1800

**BONZO DOG DOO-DAH BAND**
'I'm The Urban Spaceman' / 'Canyons Of Your Mind'
McCartney produces (as Apollo C Vermouth) and performs on A-side
Released October 11 1968
UK Liberty LBF 15144
US Imperial 66345

**MARY HOPKIN**
*Postcard*
McCartney produces, plays bass, guitar
Released February 21 1969
UK Apple SAPCOR 5
US Apple ST-3351

**JACKIE LOMAX**
*Is This What You Want?*
McCartney performs on 'Sour Milk Sea'
Released March 21 1969
UK Apple SAPCOR 6
US Apple ST-3354

**MARY HOPKIN**
'Goodbye' / 'Sparrow'
McCartney produces, performs
Released March 28 1969
UK Apple APPLE 10
US Apple 1806

**BADFINGER**
'Come And Get It' / 'Rock Of All Ages'
McCartney produces, performs on A-side
Released December 5 1969
UK Apple APPLE 20
US Apple 1815

**STEVE MILLER BAND**
*Brave New World*
McCartney performs on 'My Dark Hour'
Released June 16 1969
UK Capitol EST-184
US Capitol SKAO-184

**THE FOURMOST**
'Rosetta'/ 'Just Like Before'
McCartney produces
Released February 21 1969
UK CBS 4041

**JACKIE LOMAX**
'How The Web Was Woven' / 'Thumbin' A Ride'
McCartney produces B-side
Released February 6 1970
UK Apple APPLE 23

**JAMES TAYLOR** 'Carolina In My Mind' / 'Something's Wrong'
McCartney produces
Released November 6 1970
UK Apple APPLE 32
US Apple 1805

**CARLY SIMON**
*No Secrets*
McCartney backing vocals (with Linda) on 'Night Owl'
Released November 3 1972
UK Elektra K 42127
US Elektra EKS 74082

**RINGO STARR**
*Ringo*
McCartney plays mouth sax solo on 'You're Sixteen (You're Beautiful And You're Mine)', piano, synthesiser, backing vocals on 'Six O'Clock'
Released November 23 1973
UK Apple PCTC 252
US Apple SWAL-3413

**JAMES TAYLOR**
*Walking Man*
McCartney backing vocals on 'Rock'n'Roll Is Music Now', 'Let It All Fall Down'
Released June 2 1974
UK Warner Bros. K 56402
US Warner Bros. W 2794

**THORNTON, FRANDKIN AND UNGER AND THE BIG BAND**
*Pass On This Side*
McCartney bass, backing vocals on 'God Bless California'
Released June 17 1974
US ESP ESP63019

**SCAFFOLD**
'Liverpool Lou' / 'Ten Years On After Strawberry Jam'
McCartney produces, plays Gizmo, bass, backing vocals
Released July 29 1974
US Warner Bros. 8001

**ADAM FAITH**
*I Survive*
**McCartney** plays synthesiser on 'Change', 'Never Say Goodbye', 'Goodbye', backing vocals on 'Star Song'
**Released** August 6 1974
**UK** Warner Bros. K 56054
**US** Warner Bros. BS 2791

**ROD STEWART**
*Smiler*
**McCartney** backing vocals on 'Mine For Me'
**Released** September 27 1974
**UK** Mercury 9104-001
**US** Mercury SRM-1-1017

**PEGGY LEE**
*Let's Love*
**McCartney** produces, plays piano on 'Let's Love'
**Released** October 1 1974
**US** Atlantic SD 18108

**MIKE MCGEAR**
*McGear*
**McCartney** produces, plays guitar, piano, bass, keyboards
**Released** July 4 1975
**UK** Warner Bros. K56051
**Released** October 14 1974
**US** Warner Bros. BS 2825
**CD** Rykodisc RCD10192 (features alternative version of Dance The Do)

**PEGGY LEE**
'Let's Love' / 'Always'
**McCartney** produces, plays piano on A-side
**Released** October 25 1974
**UK** Warner Bros. K 50064

**MIKE MCGEAR**
'Leave It' / 'Sweet Baby'
**McCartney** produces, plays keyboards, bass, backing vocals
**Released** October 28 1974
**US** Warner Bros. 8037

**MIKE MCGEAR**
'Sea Breezes' / 'Givin' Grease A Ride'
**McCartney** produces, plays keyboards, bass, backing vocals
**Released** February 7 1975
**UK** Warner Bros. K 16520

**MIKE MCGEAR**
'Dance The Do' / 'Norton'
**McCartney** produces, plays keyboards, bass, backing vocals
**Released** July 4 1975
**UK** Warner Bros. K 16573

**RINGO STARR**
*Ringo's Rotogravure*
**McCartney** performs on 'Pure Gold'
**Released** September 17 1976
**UK** Polydor 2302 040
**US** Atlantic 82417-2

**ROY HARPER**
*Bullinamingvase*
**McCartney** backing vocals on 'One Of Those Days In England (Parts 2-10)'
**Released** February 11 1977
**UK** Harvest SHSP 4060

**DENNY LAINE**
*Holly Days*
**McCartney** produces, plays drums, bass, guitar, backing vocals
**Released** May 6 1977
**UK** EMI EMA 781
**Released** May 19 1977
**US** Capitol 11588 ST
**CD** Magic 3930035, February 2001

# BIBLIOGRAPHY

Badman, Keith: The Beatles After The Break -Up, Omnibus Press, 2001.
Balls, Richard: Sex & Drugs & Rock 'N' Roll: The Life Of Ian Dury, Omnibus Press, 2000.
Black, Johnny: Recording Sgt Pepper, Tracks, 1997.
Blake, John: All You Needed Was Love, Hamlyn,1983.
Blake, Peter: About Collage, Tate Gallery Publishing, 2000.
Brown, Peter & Gaines, Steven: The Love You Make, Pan, 1975.
Carr, Tony & Tyler, Tony: The Beatles An Illustrated Record, New English Library, 1991.
Clayson, Alan: Ringo Starr Straight Man Or Joker, Sidgwick & Jackson, 1990.
Clayson, Alan: The Quiet One A Life of George Harrison, Sidgwick & Jackson, 1995.
Coleman, Ray: McCartney Yesterday & Today, Boxtree, 1984.
Coleman, Ray: John Winston Lennon, Sidgwick & Jackson, 1984.
Coleman, Ray: John Ono Lennon, Sidgwick & Jackson, 1995.
Connolly, Ray: In The Sixties, Pavilion Books, 1976.
Cowan, Philip: Behind The Beatles Songs, Polytantric Press, unknown.
Davis, Andy: The Beatles Files, Bramley Books, 1995.
Eikelenboom, Edward, Oobu Joobu - A Track-By-Track Analysis Of His American Radio Show, Dutch Paul McCartney Fan Club, 1998.
Englehardt, Kristopher: Beatles Undercover, Collectors Guide Publishing, 1986. Evans, Mike: The Art Of The Beatles, Anthony Bond, 1984.
Fields, Danny: Linda McCartney: The Biography, Little, Brown & Company, 1991.
Giuliano, Geoffrey: The Beatles A Celebration, Stigwick & Jackson, 1982.
Giuliano, Geoffrey: Tomorrow Never Knows, Paper Tiger, 1977.
Goldman, Albert: The Lives Of John Lennon, Bantam Press, 1988.
Green, Jonathan: All Dressed Up: The Sixties and the Counterculture, Pimlico, 1992.
Green, Jonathan: Days in The Life: Voices from the English Underground 1961-1971, Pimlico, 1994.
Harrison, George: / Me Mine, W H Allen, 1994.
Jasper, Tony: Paul McCartney and Wings, Octopus Books Ltd, 1977.
Lewishon, Mark: The Beatles Live, Pavillon, 1997.
Lewisohn, Mark: The Complete Beatles Recording Sessions, Hamlyn, 1977.
Lewisohn, Mark: The Complete Beatles Chronicle, Pryamid Books, 1989.
MacDonald, Ian: Revolution In The Head, Forth Estate, 1984.
Madinger, Chip & Easter, Mark: Eight Arms To Hold You, 44.4, 2000.
Martin, George: Summer Of Love The Making Of Sgt Pepper, Macmillan, 1983.
Marwick, Arthur: The Sixties, Oxford University Press, 1998.
McCartney, Paul: Paintings, Little Brown, 1999.
McGear, Mike: Thank You Very Much, Arthur Baker Limited, London, 1981.
Miles: The Beatles In Their Own Words, Omnibus, 1978.
Pawlowski, Gareth: How They Became The Beatles, Macdonald,1990.
Rice, Jo & Tim: Guinness Book of Hit Singles, Guinness, 1999.
Schaffner, Nicholas: The Beatles Forever, McGraw Hill, 1978.
Standard, Neville: The Beatles The Long & Winding Road -A History Of The Beatles On Record, Virgin Books, 1982.
Standard, Neville: The Beatles Working Class Heroes, Virgin Books, 1983. The Beatles: Anthology, Cassell & Co, 2000.
Tremlett, George: The Paul McCartney Story, Futura Publications Ltd, 1975.
Turner, Steve: A Hard Days Write, Carlton, 1994.

## NEWSPAPERS, MAGAZINES AND JOURNALS
Beatles Monthly
Beatles Now.
Beatles Unlimited.
Beatlology Magazine.
Billboard.
Classic FM Magazine, August 1997 and March 2000.
Daily Mail.
Life, Vol. 90, No 12, 22 September 1967.
Music Week.
Mojo, No 35, October 1996, No 45, August 1997, No 49, December 1997, No 59, October 1998, No 62, January 1999, No 71, October 1999, No 74, January 2000, No 81, August 2000, No 83, October 2000, No 92, July 2001.
New Statesman, 26 September 1997.
OK, 6 March 1998.
P.E.T.A. Animal Times, Autumn 1998.
OK magazine, The Beatles, Band of The Century, 1999.
Radio Times, 25-31 March 1989, 13-19 June 1992, 17-23 April 1999 and 19-25 May 2001.
Record Collector, February 1986, January 1990.
Record Mirror, 24 April 1982.
Rolling Stone, 15 June 1989, 8 February 1990.
The Independent, 7 July 1997, 15 October 1997.
The Nashville Banner, 23 May, 7 and 17 June, 18 July 1974.
The Tennessean, 10, 20 and 24 May, 7, 17 and 18 June, 18, 21 July 1974.
TV Times, 14-20 August 1982, 10-16 December 1983, 13-19 October 1984, 21-27 November 1987 and 30 May-5 June 1987
USA Today, interview by Edna Gundersen.
USA Weekend, interview with Chrissie Hynde.

Vox, July 1991.
Woman's Own, 29 September 1984.

**TOUR PROGRAMMES**
Wings Over Europe.
UK Tour 1976.
UK Tour 1979.
Japan Tour 1980.
World Tour 1989/90.
New World Tour.
Liverpool Oratorio.
Music For Montserrat.
a Garland for Linda.
Working Classical.

**AUDIO VISUAL SOURCES**
Interview with Anthony Cherry, BBC Radio.
Interview with Leslie Ash — The Tube, Channel 4, 1983.
Interview with Melvin Bragg —The Making of Paul McCartney's Broad Street, ITV, 1984.
Interview with Selina Scott — BBC Breakfast News, BBC Television, 1986.
Interview with Terry Wogan, BBC Television, 1987.
Interview with Jonathan Ross — The Last Resort, Channel 4, 1987.
Interview with Bob Harris — Knebworth, BBC Radio, 1990.
Interview with Oprah Winfry SKY Television, 1997.
Interview with Chris Evans — TFI Friday, Channel 4, 1997.
Interview with Johnny Vaughn — The Big Breakfast, Channel 4, 1999.
Interview with Michael Parkinson, BBC Television, 1999.
Interview with Mark Lawson Front Row BBC Radio May, 2001.
Jools Holland interview with Chas Jankel and Laurie Latham, BBC Radio, 2001
Flaming Pie Special, BBC Television.
Paul McCartney Ghosts From The Past, BBC Television. Routes Of Rock, BBC Radio, 1999.
SFX Magazine. Issues 11 and 12, 1982.
Star Sound Extra, BBC Radio.
The Beatles Anthology, Apple.
Paul McCartney and Wings Rock Show, PMI.
Paul McCartney Once Upon A Video, PMI.
Paul McCartney Get Back, PMI.
Linda McCartney Landscapes, BBC Television.
Paul McCartney on The Roxy, ITV Television.
Wingspan, MPL.
Top Of The Pops Two - McCartney Special, BBC Television.
Band on The Run —The Story Of Wings Pt 1 and 2, BBC Radio.

**WEB-SITES**
Paul McCartney FAQ, www.macca-faq.com.
Plugged 'Harald Gernhart's' Unofficial Paul McCartney Page, cip2.e-technik.uni-erlangen.de:8080/hyplan/gernhard/macca/index.html.
Christopher Brewer's McCartney recording sessions, rgo.simplenet.com/macca. David Adcock's Paul McCartney Page, www.geocities.com/SunsetStrip/Towers/6264/macca.html.
MPL, www.mplcommunications.com.
Standing Stone, www.standingstone97.com.
Flaming Pie, www.flamingpie.com.
Macca Central, www.macca-central.com.
Wingspan, www.paulmccartney.com.
Linda McCartney Pro Cycling Team, www.lindamccartey-pct.co.uk.

**WORKS CITED**
Comments made by Paul McCartney which appear in this book have been taken from the following sources:
Bennahum, David: In Their Own Words The Beatles After The Break Up, Omnibus Press, 1981.
DiLello, Richard: The Longest Cocktail Party, Mojo Books, 2000.
Gambaccini, Paul: Paul McCartney In His Own Words, Omnibus Press, 1991.
Giuliano, Geoffrey & Brenda: The Lost Beatles Interviews, Virgin Books, 1988.
Giuliano, Geoffrey: Blackbird: The Life And Times Of Paul McCartney, Dutton, 1986.
Jasper, Tony: Paul McCartney And Wings, Octopus, 1978.
McCartney, Paul: Paintings, Exhibition Catalogue, 1994.
Miles, Barry: The Beatles In Their Own Words, Omnibus Press, 1998.
Miles, Barry: Paul McCartney: Many Years From Now, Secker and Warburg, 1999.
Pascall, Jeremy: Paul McCartney And Wings, Phoebus, 1977.
Perry, George (Ed): Paul McCartney's Broad Street, Pavilion Books, 1984.

## NEWSPAPERS, MAGAZINES AND JOURNALS

Bassist, February 2000, interview by Roger Newell.
Beatlology Magazine, Vol.3 No 5 May/June 2001.
Beatles Monthly.
Billboard, March 2001, interview with Timothy White.
Classic FM Magazine, April 2000, interview with David Thomas.
Club Sandwich The Magazine of the Paul McCartney Fun Club.
Daily Mail.
Guitar Player, July 1990, interview by Tom Mulhern.
Guitar World, October 1997, interview by Neil McCormick.
Guitarist, February 2000.
Hotwired Inc.
Insight, Issue 14, interview by Andrew Vaughan.
Life, Vol. 70, No 14, April 16 1971, interview by Richard Merymen.
Melody Maker.
Mojo, No 72, November 1999.
Musician, No 139, May 1990.
The Best of Musician, 1988, interview by Vic Garbarini.
New Musical Express, 29 April 1978 and 12 January 1980.
New Statesman, 26 September 1997.
OK, 15 November 2001.
Playboy, interview by Joan Goodman.
Q magazine, October 1986, July 1986, October 1993, December 1995 and June 1997.
Readers Digest, November 2001.
Record Collector, May 2001.
Rolling Stone, No 295, 12 July 1979, No 554, 15 June 1989 and No 571, 8 February 1990.
Scottish Daily Record.
Sounds.
Time.
The Times .
Trouser Press, interview by Ray Bonici.

## AUDIO VISUAL SOURCES

Desert Island Discs, BBC Radio.
Tug Of War Radio Special, BBC Radio.
McCartney on McCartney parts 1 - 8, BBC Radio.
Flaming Pie Radio Special, BBC Radio.
Off The Ground Radio Special, Independent Radio.
Paul McCartney Up Close, BBC Television.
Press To Play Radio Special, BBC Radio.
Interview with Andy Peebles 1980, BBC Radio.
Interview with Bob Geldorf, Triple M, Adelaide, Australia 1993.
Interview with Jody Denberg, KGSR Texas, 7 November 1999.
Interview with Nicky Horne, Capital Radio 1981, Capital Radio.
Interview with Richard Skinner - McCartney, BBC Television.
Interview on Good Morning America May 2001.
Interview with Terry Gross on Fresh Air April 30, 2001
Interview with Matt Lauer, The Today Show, NBC Television July 1997.

# Index

# Also available

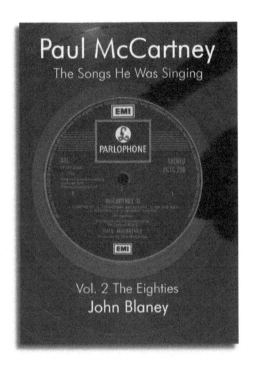

Printed in October 2023
by Rotomail Italia S.p.A., Vignate (MI) - Italy